PUFFIN BOOKS

# UNCODED: A TECHNOLOGICAL HISTORY OF INDEPENDENT INDIA

Meghaa Gupta's exploits in history are the outcome of an irrepressible urge to contextualize the challenges of the present with the past and make greater sense of the times we live in. She works in children's publishing and firmly believes that all change begins with getting children to read books that demystify the world and its infinite possibilities. She curates the Nature Writing for Children Programme at Azim Premji University and is the co-founder of Literature across Borders, an international literary exchange programme for young people's books at Bath Spa University in the UK.

Meghaa is the author of two other widely acclaimed books on independent India published by Puffin, *Unearthed: An Environmental History of Independent India* (2020) and *After Midnight: A History of Independent India* (2022). This is the third book in the series.

I0893567

## ADVANCE PRAISE FOR THE BOOK

'In a world of fast takes and fleeting attention, *Uncoded* is a quiet act of defiance. It reminds us that India's story is not only political or cultural. It is also deeply technological. And that story, for an entire generation raised on Netflix, remains largely untold. Meghaa Gupta rewires how we think of nation-building. She shows how India's post-Independence rise was stitched together through steel plants, space missions, public data systems, and sheer conviction. For any young Indian who wants to understand where we came from, and how we have held our ground, this is essential reading.'

—**Charles Assisi**, technology columnist at *Hindustan Times*, co-author of *The Aadhaar Effect: Why the World's Largest Identity Project Matters* and co-founder at Founding Fuel Pvt. Ltd

'This accessible introduction offers young readers a broad glimpse into the world of technology in India.'

—**Dinesh C. Sharma**, author of *Indian Innovation, Not Jugaad*

# UNCODED

## A TECHNOLOGICAL HISTORY OF INDEPENDENT INDIA

MEGHAA GUPTA

ILLUSTRATIONS BY SAYAN MUKHERJEE

PUFFIN BOOKS

An imprint of Penguin Random House

PUFFIN BOOKS

Puffin Books is an imprint of the Penguin Random House group of companies whose addresses can be found at global.penguinrandomhouse.com

Published by Penguin Random House India Pvt. Ltd
4th Floor, Capital Tower 1, MG Road,
Gurugram 122 002, Haryana, India

Penguin Random House India

First published in Puffin Books by Penguin Random House India 2025



10 9 8 7 6 5 4 3 2 1



ISBN 9780143467090

Book design and layout by Samar Bansal
Typeset in Charter BT Pro by Manipal Technologies Limited, Manipal
Printed at Replika Press Pvt. Ltd, India



www.penguin.co.in

MIX
Paper | Supporting responsible forestry
FSC™ C016779

*To India and its people . . .*

*The development of a nation is intimately linked with the understanding and application of science and technology by its people.*

—Vikram Ambalal Sarabhai

# Contents

# Foreword

A few years ago, I visited the National Museum of Scotland in Edinburgh. As I moved through its galleries on colonial encounters, one exhibit made me pause. It featured depictions of Tipu Sultan and the Siege of Seringapatam. These were grand oil paintings and a woven tapestry capturing the dramatic moment when British forces stormed the fort.

What truly caught my eye, though, was not just the artwork. It was a small description beside it that spoke of something remarkable: Tipu Sultan's use of iron-cased rockets in battle. These rockets astonished the British with their range and impact. It was a military technology far ahead of its time.

Tipu Sultan, who ruled from 1782 to 1799, had inherited these rocket systems from his father, Haider Ali, and refined them. Unlike anything the British had seen, these were among the world's first military rockets with metal cylinders that offered greater range and stability. After Tipu's fall in 1799, British engineers took note, studied the designs and later developed their own version—the Congreve rockets—that were used in European wars and even in the war of 1812 between the United States and the British Empire.

Standing in that museum, far away from home, I felt a quiet surge of pride and a deep reflection. Here was a reminder that for much of human history, India had been the global leader in science and technology. Not just in ancient times but right up to the eighteenth century, our civilization stood at the forefront of innovation. We pioneered advances in mathematics, astronomy, metallurgy, medicine and engineering. We built observatories and universities, charted planetary movements, performed complex surgeries, and yes, even launched rockets.

The decline that followed was not the result of fading genius. It came from a deliberate, systematic dismantling of our institutions, our industries and our intellectual ecosystems under colonial rule. Knowledge was extracted. Confidence was eroded. Generations were taught to forget what had once been possible.

Yet, the truth does not vanish. It lingers in artefacts, forgotten footnotes and in memories waiting to be reawakened.

This book is about reigniting memory. It takes us back into the past, so we can move forward with purpose.

Through vivid storytelling and meticulous research, Meghaa Gupta takes us on a remarkable journey through India's modern technological evolution. She begins in the early years after Independence, when electricity was a luxury in many villages, and follows the arc to today, when India is launching satellites, building indigenous fighter jets and exporting cutting-edge missile systems.

One chapter that particularly stood out to me was the one on India's journey to build the Electronic Voting Machine (EVM). Far more than just a piece of hardware, the EVM emerged from a deep democratic need to make elections more transparent, scalable and inclusive in a country as vast and diverse as ours. Meghaa shows us how this innovation was not born in labs alone but shaped by policy thinkers, engineers and on-ground challenges. The chapter captures how technology, when rooted in democratic values, can transform not just a system but a society.

Another chapter recounts the humble beginnings of India's space programme, which did not start with billion-dollar labs, but in a small church in Thumba. Rocket parts were carried on bicycles. Engineers assembled them by hand. From those modest first steps, we have reached the Moon, touched Mars, and are now preparing for Gaganyaan, our first human spaceflight mission.

Yet, beyond the machines and missions, this book is really about people. Meghaa introduces us to scientists, women engineers, rural innovators, teachers and dreamers. These are the everyday heroes who carried the vision of a modern India, quietly, tirelessly and with unwavering resolve.

That is what makes *Uncoded* so powerful. It isn't just a story of technology; it is a story of resilience, imagination and the belief that even against impossible odds, progress is possible.

Today, as India stands on the brink of a new technological age, whether it is space exploration, digital infrastructure, clean energy or strategic defence, we have every reason to be optimistic. However, true momentum will come not from machines, but from minds. From our children. They are the changemakers, the future scientists, coders, doctors and engineers. And books like *Uncoded* are more than just history lessons. They are invitations for young minds to ask questions, to imagine bold futures and to believe in their ability to shape the world.

I hope every young Indian who reads this book feels a spark of curiosity, of pride and of purpose. Because we have led before. And with courage, creativity and clarity, we will lead again.

Srijan Pal Singh
Author, education innovator and social entrepreneur
Founder and mentor, Dr. A.P.J Abdul Kalam Centre
June, 2025

# Introduction

My grandparents grew up in the 1940s, in an India without electricity.

My parents grew up in the 1960s, in an India without colour televisions or personal computers.

I grew up in the 1980s and early 1990s, in an India without mobile phones.

And today? Children are reportedly using artificial intelligence to do their schoolwork!

In the years since Independence, India has undergone an incredible technological transformation. Yet, in 1947, few could have imagined such a future.

Back then, India was a largely rural country, burdened by poverty, illiteracy, hunger and disease. It had more problems than means to overcome them.

To make matters even more challenging, it was born into a world that had just witnessed the most destructive war in human history. Astonishing new technologies—from computers to radars—developed and used during World War II were reshaping life across the globe, and India's leaders didn't want their country to be left behind.

So, with dreams in their eyes and an abiding resolve, a small band of visionary policymakers, scientists and industrialists embarked on an ambitious quest to bring technological progress to the nation.

Newly independent India lacked the knowledge to build the technologies it needed and getting them from abroad wasn't always possible. Countries that owned some of the most powerful technologies of the time weren't always willing to share them.

Yet, India refused to give up. Instead, it found its own ways of imagining, building and using modern technology.

Slowly but surely, things began to change . . .

Giant dams came up on large rivers, diverting water for farms and power plants. Electricity lit up more lives, and education opened up more minds to science and technology. Factories began to churn out everything from gleaming steel to cars and cutlery. Scrapyards were scoured for materials to build computers. Rockets were carried on bicycles before being launched into space. Mexican wheat was made 'chapati-ready' to fight crippling food shortages. All kinds of imported technologies—from missiles to medicines—were reverse-engineered to manufacture them locally. Roadways began to criss-cross the country, connecting more places, and cars became easier to spot.

Today, India's technological achievements are recognized globally. It is the birthplace of some of the biggest software companies on the planet and its space programme is among the best in the world. For many Indians, modern technology has become part of daily life. At the click of a button, we can connect with someone across the globe, attend a class, order a meal, book a cab or stream a movie.

Technology, however, is ever-changing and keeping up with it is a formidable challenge. Even as I write this introduction, artificial intelligence seems to be conquering the world, and people warn me of its dangers. I am told that it will take away many jobs, including mine.

Sometimes I worry: what will the increasing capabilities of technology mean for us humans who create and use it? My worries are intensified by the wars and violence in the news and how countries are using different technologies to annihilate each other.

But looking back at independent India's technological journey has taught me that such fears have always been with us—and, somehow, we have always found a way out.

*Uncoded: A Technological History of Independent India* is a story of how a young and struggling nation used science and technology to dream big, build boldly and carve out a future that once seemed impossible. In reading it, I hope you discover that what matters more than the power of technology is what we choose to do with it.

Meghaa
June, 2025

# Stuck in Time

On 1 September 1939, German forces invaded Poland, beginning a war that we know as World War II. On one side of this terrifying war were Germany, Italy and Japan, together known as the Axis powers. On the other side were the Allies—Great Britain, the Soviet Union or the USSR (now Russia), the United States of America (USA) and a few other countries. Over the next six years, both sides fought fierce battles across Europe, Africa and the Asia-Pacific region.

More than anything else, World War II was a chilling display of scientific and technological prowess. Scientists, especially in Germany, Britain and the USA, developed numerous technologies that changed the future: computers that took only minutes to break codes containing secret messages; radar technology that detected objects located at a great distance using invisible radio waves; superfast aircraft that rained fire from the skies; and supersonic rockets that travelled hundreds of kilometres, demolishing large areas and killing thousands of people in a single blow.

However, the invention that sent shockwaves through the world was the nuclear bomb, made by a team of American scientists led by J. Robert Oppenheimer. In August 1945, when

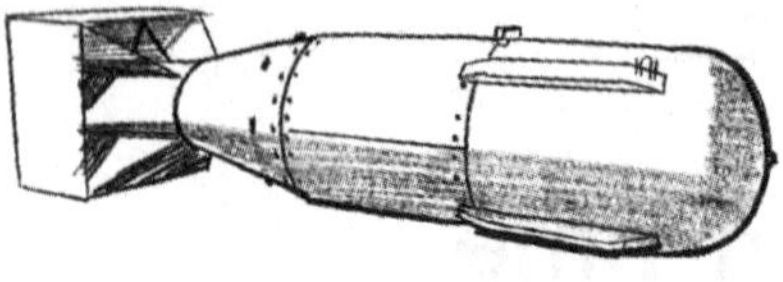

Little Boy

Fat Man

two nuclear bombs, codenamed Little Boy and Fat Man, were dropped on the Japanese cities of Hiroshima and Nagasaki, the world witnessed just how frightening technology could be. The explosions that followed sent up monstrous mushroom clouds into the atmosphere and set off raging firestorms that annihilated everything on the ground for several kilometres. Shaken by the bombings, Japan surrendered. The Axis powers had finally been defeated by the Allies.

Mushroom cloud rising over Nagasaki

By September 1945, World War II had come to an end, but it had pushed the world into a dark and anxious age. Most countries were worried. What if a nuclear bomb were dropped on them next? Heightening this tension was the Cold War—an intense rivalry that began between the USA and the Soviet Union, the two leading superpowers at the end of World War II. From weapons to spacecraft, both the superpowers scrambled to corner the most powerful technologies for themselves and wield greater influence over the world.

But where was India in the middle of this full-fledged race for scientific and technological might?

## India's Story

At the beginning of World War II, Britain ruled over the largest empire the world had ever seen. It spread over nearly a quarter of the globe, including India. By the end of the war, though, Britain had been significantly weakened and could no longer exert the same amount of power over its empire as it once had. A majority of its people wanted Britain to focus its resources on rebuilding itself instead of retaining its hold over foreign lands.

In the elections held in Britain in 1945, a new political party headed by Clement Atlee came to power, and it decided to immediately implement the wishes of the British people. Bit by bit, the British Empire dissolved, and the countries ruled by it awoke to much-awaited freedom. The first among these was India, which had been passionately demanding independence for several decades under the leadership of Mohandas Karamchand Gandhi—a man whose emphasis on non-violence made people call him *mahatma* (meaning a 'noble soul'). But the India that awoke to freedom on 15 August 1947 would be barely recognizable today.

At the time of Independence, most Indians lived in villages, worked on farms and had never heard of electricity. Used to doing their work by hand, they were largely oblivious to modern machines. Many of their leaders also mistrusted modern technology. Mahatma Gandhi famously said:

> 'Today machinery merely helps a few to ride on the backs of millions. The impetus behind it all is not . . . to save labour, but greed.'

### The Japanese Way

In 1868, Japan, which had never been conquered by any Western power, saw the rise of Emperor Meiji. He overthrew the reigning medieval warlords and began to modernize the largely agricultural country. By the time of his death in 1912, Japan had a well-developed transport and communication system and rapidly growing industries based on the latest technology, among other modern amenities. Long before Independence, many Indian leaders, such as Pandit Madan Mohan Malaviya, had identified Japan's rapid technological advancement as a possible model for independent India to follow.

Despite this resistance, it was hard to deny the dominant role of science and technology in modern life across the world. Jawaharlal Nehru, who became the first prime minister of independent India, did not want his country to fall behind. Yet, how this technological advancement should proceed was a matter of deep debate.

## The Technology Question

Some renowned politicians, engineers and businessmen, including Madan Mohan Malaviya, Mokshagundam Visvesvaraya and J.R.D. Tata wanted India to rapidly adopt modern machines for development. But at the time of Independence, India did not have sufficient technological expertise and capabilities of its own. It needed to get these from foreign countries, which required a lot of money, and India did not have enough to spare. Moreover, after centuries of British rule, many of its leaders were wary of depending excessively on foreign countries to meet India's technological needs. Besides, most of its people were poor and uneducated, and Nehru was worried that the newness of modern technology would overwhelm them. It would also threaten livelihoods by taking away many jobs that had so far been done by hand. Quite apart from these issues, he was concerned that the conveniences of modern technology would make people slaves to machines and limit their social interactions.

With these thoughts in mind, Nehru and a motley group of scientists and planners set out on a cautious and deliberate programme of technological advancement for India.

## Makers of Modern India

The story of independent India's technological march began with a handful of distinguished scientists and technologists who dared to dream despite the monetary and technological limitations they faced in their work.

### Father of Research Laboratories in India

S.S. BHATNAGAR

A chemist and academic, Shanti Swarup Bhatnagar played a key role in establishing the Council of Scientific and Industrial Research (CSIR), India's leading scientific research institution, in 1942 and setting up twelve laboratories under it. These laboratories, such as the National Physical Laboratory, the National Chemical Laboratory and the National Metallurgical Laboratory, played an important role in researching and developing technologies beneficial for India's industrial development.

### Father of Indian Statistics

P.C. MAHALANOBIS

A statistician, Prasanta Chandra Mahalanobis established the Indian Statistical Institute (ISI) in Calcutta (now Kolkata) in 1931. Under his leadership, it became one of the world's leading institutes to study statistics—the science of collecting, organizing and analysing information or data. The ISI designed and implemented the National Sample Survey, which collected crucial social and economic data that India needed to plan its development.

### Father of India's Nuclear Programme

A physicist, Homi Jehangir Bhabha set up the Tata Institute of Fundamental Research (TIFR) in 1945 to carry out research in nuclear science. Nine years later, in 1954, he set up the Atomic Energy Establishment at Trombay to develop nuclear energy.

HOMI BHABHA

### Father of India's Space Programme

A physicist and industrialist, Vikram Ambalal Sarabhai laid the foundation of space research in India by setting up the Indian National Committee for Space Research (INCOSPAR) in 1962. This organization later became the Indian Space Research Organisation (ISRO).

VIKRAM SARABHAI

**A Question for Readers:** Did you notice what unites the scientists and technologists mentioned here? They are all men (fathers!).

Historically, the fields of science, technology, engineering and mathematics (STEM) have been dominated by men because many people believed women were incapable of pursuing these subjects. Educational institutions restricted them from studying STEM, and if they did manage to study these subjects, workplaces often discriminated against them. Despite these odds, many women have chosen to pursue STEM. Look out for them throughout this book and find out about others.

## India in the Cold War

The Cold War between the USA and the Soviet Union was a war of ideologies—both the superpowers had very different ideas about how countries should be run. The USA promoted democracy, letting people elect their government from among various political parties, whereas the Soviet Union (now Russia) followed communism, where a single political party was in charge, and people did not have the opportunity to vote for any other.

Each superpower championed its own ideology, leaving India with a tough choice: whose side should it take? India had chosen to be a democracy. As such, it could have sided with the USA. However, it was determined to preserve its newfound independence and refused to do this. Instead, in 1961, Nehru, the then prime minister of India, joined Josip Broz Tito of Yugoslavia (now divided into several independent countries), Gamal Abdel Nasser of Egypt, Kwame Nkrumah of Ghana and Sukarno of Indonesia to officially establish the Non-Aligned Movement—an international group of countries that neither aligned with, nor stood against, any superpower.

The superpowers responded to this by waging a contest over who could exert greater influence on the non-aligned nations. As the largest country in South Asia and a former territory of Britain—a close ally of the USA—India became a significant battleground in this contest. It tried to make the best of this situation without compromising its non-aligned stance. During the 1950s, under the Colombo Plan for Cooperative Economic Development in South and South-east Asia, India became one of the biggest beneficiaries of technical and financial assistance from Britain and other countries in the American bloc. Among the greatest legacies of this plan was that it helped train thousands of Indian engineers and scientists in crucial fields like agriculture, medicine and mechanics through international exchange programmes and collaborations. However, this did not stop India from securing assistance from the Soviet Union as well.

Being able to get help from both the superpowers without aligning with either not only propelled India's technological progress in the early decades after Independence but also increased its credibility among other non-aligned countries.

## On the Road to Transformation

Giant factories producing all manner of goods, countless cars on the streets, mobile phones in most hands . . . today technology seems omnipresent in India. But the road to this advancement was long and complicated.

For several decades, modern technology remained too expensive and distant for the majority of Indians. But things began to change as more and more people engaged with modern machines and learned new ways of doing things. A most remarkable transformation was in the making.

## PART 1

# THE MARCH OF MODERN TECHNOLOGY

# 1

# Laying the Foundation

During the sixteenth century, India was one of the richest countries in the world. From Europe to Southeast Asia, its products, particularly its exquisite hand-woven cotton cloth, were prized in many countries. So, it wasn't surprising that traders from all over the world came to India for business.

At the beginning of the seventeenth century, British traders from the newly established East India Company came calling. Like everyone else, they too were interested in Indian products. Bit by bit, their influence increased as they fought off their rivals and gained control over India. Meanwhile, back in Britain, something extraordinary began to unfold.

Inspired by modern science, clever inventors built machines that could work faster and more efficiently than people. Soon, activities like spinning and weaving that had long been done by hand came to be done by machines in bustling factories running on steam.

The hum of factories and hiss of steam announced the arrival of the Industrial Revolution that transformed Britain during the eighteenth century. It now turned to its global empire for raw materials to feed its factories and markets to sell the goods they were churning out at an astonishing rate.

With its vast natural resources and population, India seemed like the perfect place to supply both.

By the nineteenth century, India had become a supplier of raw materials for British factories. Meanwhile, India's local industries were systematically dismantled to ensure there would be no competition for the goods coming from Britain's factories. When it finally gained independence from British rule in 1947, India, which was once a land of skilled artisans and flourishing trade, had been reduced to an impoverished, underdeveloped country that made very little on its own. To produce what it needed and create more jobs for its people, newly independent India needed to set up modern factories and industrialize.

## Back to Basics

To begin with, India needed to build basic infrastructure—facilities like electricity and transportation that are essential to run factories. While the British had made significant investments in infrastructure to benefit their business in India, most of these facilities were centred around the coastal cities of Bombay (now Mumbai), Calcutta (now Kolkata) and Madras (now Chennai), which had served as important ports of trade. After Independence, the Indian government decided to expand this infrastructure throughout the country.

### Infrastructure: Then and Now

Newly independent India was relatively advanced among former British territories in terms of infrastructure. Although some of this infrastructure went to Pakistan and what is now Bangladesh, following the Partition, India has made giant strides in developing these facilities since its independence.

## Electricity

Power generation was extremely limited in British India—most things were done manually and barely any electricity was needed. However, it became one of the greatest priorities for independent India. Each state set up a system of generating, transmitting and distributing electricity, which became part of a regional and eventually a national power grid. In 2023, India was the third-largest producer of electricity in the world.

| 1947 | 2023 |
| --- | --- |
| **About 1,362 MW** of electricity generation capacity | **>4,00,000 MW** of electricity generation capacity |

Source: Central Electricity Authority, 'Growth of Electricity Sector in India from 1947–2024.'

How did people keep themselves cool in the heat when there was no electricity in India? By using hand fans or *pankhas*! In wealthy households and government buildings, giant pankhas were installed on the ceiling and pankha-pullers were hired to move these using chords connected to the contraption. All through the hot summer, the pankha-pullers were hard at work, cooling the heads of their employers. Once winter set in, the pankhas were dismantled, cleaned and put away until the next summer.

## Roadways

Building roads was a low priority for the British—there were very few motor vehicles in India, and road transport was not profitable. At the time of Independence, India hoped to build at least sixteen kilometres of roads for every 100 square kilometres of land. Having achieved this by the 1950s, it expanded its road-building activity. In 2023, India had the second-largest road network in the world.

| 1947 | 2023 |
|---|---|
| **About 4,00,000 kms** of roads | **>66,00,000 kms** of roads |

Source: Kerala Road Safety Authority, 'History of Indian Roads,' and Ministry of Road Transport & Highways, 'Year End Review 2023.'

In 2012, India completed the Golden Quadrilateral—its most extensive highway project connecting Delhi, Mumbai, Chennai and Kolkata.

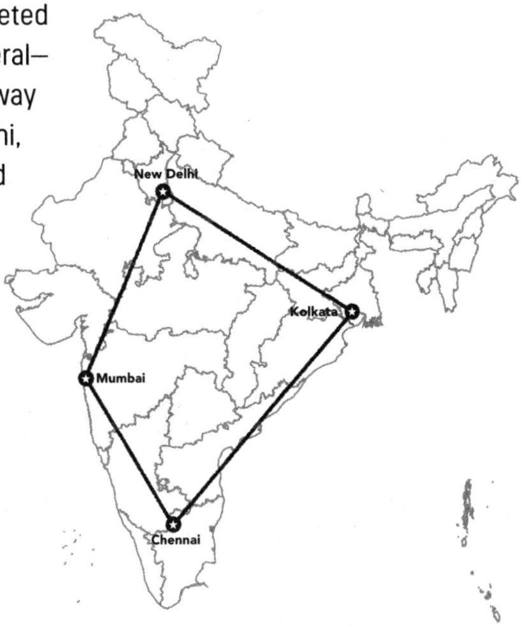


*Map not to scale

## Railways

The steam railway was the greatest legacy of the British Empire. It revolutionized transport, connecting different parts of India in ways they had never been connected before. Independent India continued to build on this and in 2023, India had the fourth-largest railway network in the world after the USA, China and Russia.

**1947**

**>50,000 kms** of railway routes

**2023**

**>68,000 kms** of railway routes

Source: Centre for Social and Economic Progress, 'Riding the Tracks of Time: Indian Railways—An Unfinished Revolution (working paper 68),' and Ministry of Finance, 'Economic Survey 2023–24.'

Launched in 2018, Vande Bharat was the first modern trainset designed and built in India. It marked India's entry into an elite group of trainset manufacturers.

## Postal System

At the time of Independence, most post offices in India were situated in urban areas. Since then, the postal network has expanded extensively, reaching almost every corner of rural India, and has become the largest network in the world.

| 1947 | 2023 |
|---|---|
| **>23,000** post offices | **>1,55,000** post offices |

Source: India Post, 'Post Office Network.'

First postal stamp issued by independent India on 21 November 1947.

## Embracing Science

Education levels in India at the time of Independence were extremely low, and most people blindly believed in age-old ideas and superstitions that made them discriminate against each other based on gender, caste and religion. A society steeped in such thinking had, for instance, considered girls and people belonging to the so-called lower castes unworthy of an education for the longest time. Many Indian social reformers, scientists and leaders such as B.R. Ambedkar and Jawaharlal Nehru opposed such thinking. The world into which independent India was born had been shaped by the power of science, and India's scientists and leaders wanted its people to adopt a 'scientific temper'. They wanted Indians to understand the world by observing it, questioning what they saw, and reasoning.

The best way to promote a scientific temper was to educate people in science and technology. Independent India had inherited a set of scientific institutions, such as the Indian Institute of Science (IISc), the Indian Statistical Institute (ISI), the Council for Scientific and Industrial Research (CSIR) and the Tata Institute of Fundamental Research (TIFR), which were already conducting education programmes and carrying out research necessary for development. As prime minister, Jawaharlal Nehru oversaw a golden age in Indian science, establishing various major research laboratories, national and regional engineering colleges and technical institutes. Among these were the famous Indian Institutes of Technology (IITs), modelled after the Massachusetts Institute of Technology (MIT) in the US. The first IIT was established at Kharagpur, West Bengal, in 1951.

Nehru's quest for scientific temper was not restricted to establishing education and research institutions. He placed great emphasis on training Indian engineers working on nation-building projects. Furthermore, he wanted scientists and engineers working on such projects to spread their knowledge by educating ordinary workers about the purpose and significance of their labour.

### Make a Trip

India has one of the world's largest formal networks of science museums and centres. The first of these was the Birla Museum, established in 1959 on the campus of the Birla Institute of Technology and Science (BITS) in Pilani, Rajasthan.

## The First Factories

Having made a start at developing basic facilities and promoting scientific education and research, India began to industrialize in a big way from 1956. Initially, it focused on basic industries such as iron and steel, which produced the raw materials needed by several other sectors, such as construction and heavy machinery. At the time of Independence, India had two steel plants—the Tata Iron and Steel Company in Jamshedpur and the Indian Iron and Steel Company in Burnpur—which produced just over 10 lakh tonnes a year. This was not enough for India's needs.

With an initial aim of producing 60 lakh tonnes of steel, the government decided to set up new steel plants. All of these were to come up in and around Central India, which was rich in iron ore and coal—key ingredients in manufacturing steel.

Given its technological deficit, India invited help from foreign countries. Various industrialized countries entered a lively contest to win an invitation. Eventually, Germany, Britain and the Soviet Union (now Russia) signed agreements to help build steel plants at Rourkela in Orissa (now Odisha),

Durgapur in West Bengal and Bhilai in Madhya Pradesh (now in Chhattisgarh), respectively.

In a world plagued by the Cold War between the USA and the Soviet Union, it was significant that the Americans had failed to win an invitation to build one of the first steel plants in independent India. A gleeful Soviet media ran lavish photos of the project at Bhilai as a symbol of Indo-Soviet cooperation. The Soviet leader, Nikita Khrushchev, compared Bhilai to Magnitogorsk, a major industrial city in Russia.

In these steel factories, Indians worked shoulder to shoulder with foreigners, laying the foundation of independent India's industrial future. The foreign partners provided the machinery and the training for Indian engineers and technicians. Many of them were sent abroad for further training. Some industries also set up training schools on their premises to equip the workforce with the necessary skills to work in the factories. This furthered Nehru's aspiration for scientific temper.

In 1959, the first flush of steel came out of Bhilai. For those working in the factory, this was one of the most exciting moments of their lives. The steel factory was proof that India was no longer a backward country. Slowly, but surely, it was joining the march of industrial progress. But the path to this progress was laid with countless challenges.

## Factories Far and Wide

In British India, most industries were situated in and around the coastal cities of Bombay (now Mumbai), Calcutta (now Kolkata) and Madras (now Chennai). To spread industrialization, independent India began setting up industries in previously unindustrialized places like Bhopal and Tiruchirappalli (also known as Trichy). Economists might have frowned upon such idealism; setting up industries away from coastal areas created problems in transporting the imported machines and other raw materials that arrived at the coasts, thereby increasing costs. Yet, such considerations paled under the grand vision to industrialize India as a whole.

Factories were built outside cities because the land was cheaper, and fewer people would be displaced. Although these factories were not inside cities, they were close enough to offer transport for people to come to work. In many places, entire townships were built around these factories with roads, sewer systems, housing, shops, hospitals, schools and other such infrastructure. For example, in the early 1960s, Bharat Heavy Electricals Limited (BHEL), India's largest engineering and manufacturing company, set up a factory and township around twenty-six kilometres outside Hyderabad. In this way, the spread of industrialization also led to a growth in infrastructure.

## Battling the Odds

In most countries, technological advancement meant using machines to save human labour. But in a populous country like India, where labour was plentiful and cheap, it was almost always more cost-effective to hire more people instead of bringing in expensive machines for the same work. Dam building offered one of the greatest examples of this strategy. In 1947, when the US ambassador to India offered American assistance on a dam-building project, he was left rather frustrated by Nehru's insistence that the project should limit the use of machines to ensure that more unskilled workers could get jobs. The ambassador condescendingly remarked that Indians seemed 'to prefer building dams with workers carrying dirt in baskets on their heads, and to take ten years to do it'!

A much-photographed example of independent India's labour-for-machines strategy was the Nagarjuna Sagar Dam that was built on the Krishna River between modern-day Andhra Pradesh and Telangana. Thousands of labourers worked day and night, hauling stones and trays full of mortar up the face of the dam. Magazine photographers clicked pictures of this spectacle, comparing it to the construction of the pyramids in ancient Egypt!

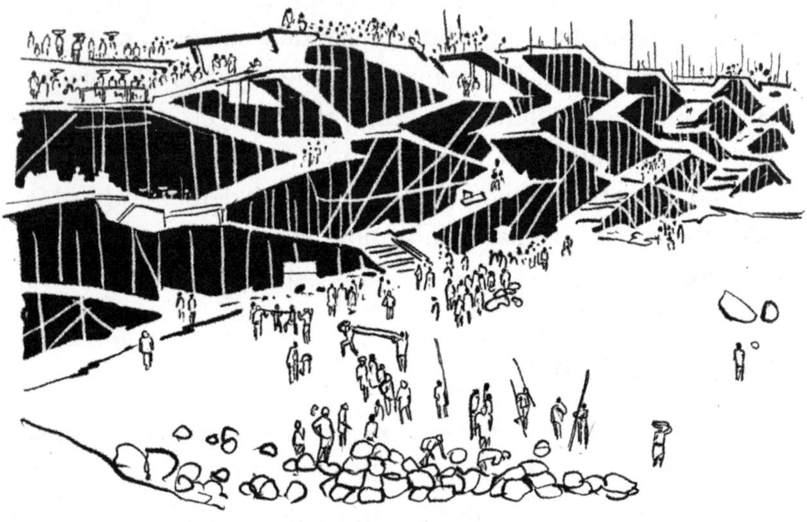

Construction of the Nagarjuna Sagar Dam

Apart from substituting machines with labour, resource-strapped industries often came up with ways to substitute one resource with another. For instance, when a heavy electrical plant in Bhopal faced a shortage of copper to make windings (coiled wires) for electric power generators, it searched for alternatives and eventually substituted copper, which needed to be imported, with locally available aluminium.

Using second-hand equipment imported from industrialized nations to save costs was another common practice in the early years. For example, the indigenous carmakers Hindustan Motors and Premier Automobiles bought second-hand production technology from European carmakers, which is why their cars closely resembled foreign models.

Launched in 1957, the Ambassador is widely considered the first Indian car. Made by Hindustan Motors, it resembled the British Morris Oxford Series III because of the use of imported production technology.

The Tata Indica, launched in the 1998, was the first truly indigenous car with nearly 98 per cent of its parts designed and manufactured in India.

## Public vs Private

In newly independent India, only the government possessed the monetary means and resources required for setting up large-scale industries such as coal, iron and steel, and heavy machinery. Most of the private sector was not powerful or wealthy enough to undertake such massive projects. Hence, most large enterprises were government-controlled (or public sector) companies. Private companies were typically engaged in making consumer goods—everything from bicycles and razor blades to refrigerators and television sets. The government protected Indian companies by imposing heavy taxes on most foreign goods. Such protection made many companies complacent because there was no competition to be wary of!

To ordinary Indians, such restrictions were most visible in the market where choices were limited, many goods were in short supply and people had to make do with whatever was available, even if it was expensive and of poor quality. The supply of some consumer goods, like scooters, fell so short that buyers often had to wait several years to receive their orders! This made many Indians develop a craze for anything new and imported.

## Troubling Times

During the 1960s and 1970s, India struggled with wars and drought. Expenses mounted, and the scarcity of resources increased. Hoping to save its fast-depleting coffers, the government tightened its grip over the economy. It took control of more industries and introduced a stringent and cumbersome system of issuing permissions (licences) to set up new private companies. Despite such measures, rescuing India's reserves proved to be an impossible challenge, and at the beginning of the 1990s, the country found itself facing an alarming economic crisis.

The new government, led by Prime Minister Narasimha Rao, that came to power at the end of the elections held in 1991 was shocked to discover that India barely had enough foreign exchange to buy three weeks' worth of much-needed imports and its borrowing had spiralled out of control! With no time left to waste, Rao immediately called upon economist Manmohan Singh to sort out the mess.

## A New India

After its independence, India strived to produce everything it needed on its own and reduce its dependence on foreign countries. To this end, the government set up a large public sector, maintained strict control over the private sector and imposed various restrictions on foreign imports and assistance. While this helped to create several industries in India, it failed to bring the promised prosperity. Instead, the country found itself saddled with many unproductive industries that neither met the needs of its people adequately nor reduced the overall dependence on foreign imports.

Manmohan Singh saw that the only way out was to change the way India had been industrializing since Independence—the government needed to reduce its control over industries and imports. To do this, he introduced ground-breaking reforms in 1991 that became a turning point in India's industrial and technological story.

Foreign goods and services were allowed to flow more easily into India, and the government stopped protecting most local industries—they needed to fight off competition on their own. The government also demolished the draconian system of issuing licenses. Instead, it invited private sector enterprises to set up new companies and even sold many public sector companies to the private sector. Encouraged by these changes, many foreign companies began to set up offices in India and invest in the country.

Many milestones in India's technological progress came in the years after 1991, when wealth increased and access to foreign technology and knowledge became easier. India established a world-renowned software industry, launched hundreds of satellites into space, and developed and exported missiles to other countries. But all these milestones came on the back of a newly independent country's monumental efforts to modernize on its own terms.

## Jugaad

The economic turmoil of the 1970s prompted the government to push small-scale, low-cost technologies made from locally available resources in a big way. It claimed that for a developing country like India, these technologies were more appropriate than large-scale industrial technologies that used up a lot of resources and often needed to be imported.

Branded as frugal innovation or *jugaad*, a Hindi word that loosely translates to 'quick fix', such technologies were not unique to India. The scarcity of resources had inspired many developing countries such as Kenya, China and Brazil to pursue their own versions of this do-more-with-less practice. But the Indian government turned jugaad into a very visible, nationwide pursuit.

Reputed academic institutions such as the IITs and the Indian Institutes of Management (IIMs) hosted seminars and set up research centres to brainstorm and identify such technologies, fuelling ideas like biogas plants that used agricultural waste to make fertilizers, mechanical bullock carts and solar handpumps. However, in the absence of sufficient funding and business interest, most such innovations could not be widely adopted. Many of them were also criticized for being impractical science projects that could not contribute to national development and technological progress in a significant way.

Early examples of jugaad included vehicles that farmers in Punjab assembled during the 1960s using discarded automobile parts, irrigation pumps and four-wheeled carts to transport people and produce over short distances.

*Imagine you are a scientist, and you have discovered something amazing, such as a material that can replace plastic or a technology that can turn seawater into drinking water. You would love to share your idea, but you are also worried—what if someone steals your idea? To prevent such a situation, scientists have long chosen to patent their discoveries. A patent is like a protective shield for new discoveries. It stops other people from copying or selling them without permission for a specified number of years. Anyone found flouting this can be taken to court.*

*One morning in 1995, when Raghunath Anant Mashelkar, the head of the CSIR in India, opened the newspaper, he was shocked to find a headline claiming that the wound-healing properties of turmeric (haldi), a popular Indian spice, had been patented by scientists in the USA! How could scientists in the USA claim to have invented something that had been common knowledge in India for generations? Not one to remain silent, Mashelkar decided he would fight this unfair patent.*

*In an NPR podcast about his 'patent war', Mashelkar revealed that such problems arose because the bodies granting patents in the West did not have easy access to sources of indigenous knowledge; so scientists could get patents for 'discoveries' based on such knowledge without difficulty. In the case of turmeric, scientists at the University of Mississippi had managed to get a patent for a particular way of using the spice to treat wounds, since the patent examiners did not have access to ancient Indian texts prescribing this treatment (they were in Sanskrit). When this was brought to the attention of patent examiners, the patent was revoked, and Mashelkar, who was already well known as The Patent Guy and Patentkar, earned another nickname—Warrior of Haldi Ghati. Eventually, more such cases of traditional and indigenous knowledge being patented in the West were discovered. The problem was so rampant that people started calling it 'biopiracy'.*

*To prevent such exploitative practices, Mashelkar began an initiative called the Traditional Knowledge Digital Library, which offered patent examiners access to India's vast reserves of indigenous knowledge in various languages, including English. Apart from protecting the country's traditional knowledge, Mashelkar's battle for patents was also an effort to inspire Indian scientists to think of their discoveries as valuable assets that they could benefit from in the global market.*

# 2

# Military Might

Non-violence had defined India's freedom struggle, and its leaders wanted the newly independent nation to preserve this peaceful tradition. But as soon as Independence arrived, India's military had to be swiftly called into action.

In 1947, British India was partitioned to create Pakistan—a separate country for Muslims. A wave of communal violence gripped the land as lakhs of Hindus and Sikhs fled Muslim-majority Pakistan while lakhs of Muslims fled Hindu-majority India. The military came to the rescue of fleeing refugees. While the army erected bridges and repaired existing roads to assist evacuation, pilots of the air force dropped aid and ferried groups of refugees in aeroplanes.

The map of colonial India in 1947 was made up of eleven provinces directly administered by the British, more than 500 princely states ruled by various nawabs and maharajas under British control and a few territories controlled by the French and the Portuguese. Post-Independence, a majority of the British provinces became part of India. Most of the princely states were situated close to Indian territory, and by Independence, a majority of them had also joined the Union of India. But trouble brewed in some corners and the military had to be deployed there too.

Although internal turmoil often led to military interventions, it was warfare that became a key driver of technological advancement in India's armed forces.

## Indian Military: Then and Now

The British Empire had built up a formidable military in pre-Independence India that not only served it within the country but also fought for it overseas. Partition divided these military forces and assets between independent India and Pakistan. In the end, India inherited basic military infrastructure that it has expanded extensively in the years since Independence.

### Ordnance Factories

(manufacturers of defence equipment)

| 1947 | 2023 |
|---|---|
| 18 | 41 |

Source: Directorate of Ordnance (Coordination and Services), 'History.'

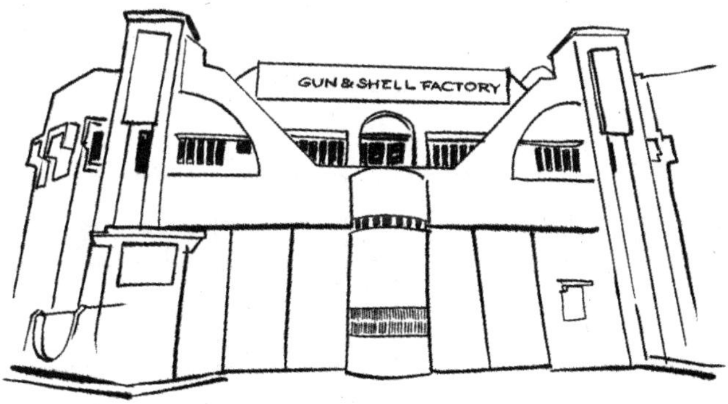


Established by the British in 1801, the Gun & Shell factory at Cossipore, Calcutta (now Kolkata) is the oldest ordnance factory in the Indian subcontinent.

## Troops on the Ground

| 1947 | 2023 |
|---|---|
| 2,80,000 approximately | 14,00,000 approximately |

Source: *India's Wars: A Military History, 1947–1971* by Arjun Subramaniam, and Brigadier Defence Academy, 'Strength of the Indian Army in 2023.'

Fondly called the *thambis* (meaning 'younger brothers' in Tamil), the Madras Regiment, established in the 1750s, is the oldest infantry regiment in the Indian army.

## Air Squadrons

(units of the air force)

| 1947 | 2023 |
|---|---|
| 8 | 31 |

Source: *A Technological History of Cold-War India, 1947–1969* by William A.T. Logan, and 'India's Fighter Jet Conundrum,' *The Hindu*.

The Indian Air Force was officially established on 8 October 1933. One of its first aircraft was the Westland Wapiti IIA, a two-seat, general-purpose military biplane (an aircraft with two sets of wings).

## Naval Force

(units of the navy)

| 1947 | 2023 |
|---|---|
| **32 ships** approximately | **150 ships and submarines** approximately |

Source: *India's Quest for Security: Defence Policies 1947–1965* by Lorne J. Kavic, and 'India's Navy Expands Fleet with Eyes on Indian Ocean Rivalry,' *Al Jazeera*.

Commissioned in 1961, INS *Vikrant* was India's first aircraft carrier. It was initially built as HMS *Hercules* for the British Royal Navy during World War II, but its construction was not completed. In 1957, the Indian navy purchased the incomplete vessel and completed its construction. The carrier remained in service for thirty-six years and played a pivotal role in the Indo-Pak war of 1971.

## War Comes Calling

Located on the northern tip of independent India, Jammu and Kashmir was a Muslim-majority princely state ruled by a Hindu maharaja, Hari Singh. It shared its borders with both India and Pakistan but wanted to remain independent. In September 1947, its relations with Pakistan began to deteriorate, and in October, a large group of armed infiltrators from across the border launched a full-fledged invasion. Unable to defend the state, Maharaja Hari Singh decided to join the Union of India on 26 October 1947. The very next day, Indian planes made their way to Kashmir with soldiers and supplies. An infuriated Pakistan ordered its troops to launch a counteroffensive. It had barely been three months since Independence, and India had already been drawn into a full-blown war.

Eventually, the United Nations (UN) intervened, and a ceasefire was ordered in January 1949. A UN commission established a Line of Control (LoC), allowing Pakistan to retain the parts of Kashmir it had occupied. Neither nation was satisfied with this solution. Pakistan had failed to conquer the entire state, while India had been stopped in its tracks and was unable to recapture the territory seized by Pakistan.

The 1947 war established Pakistan as a military threat, and India was keen to ensure that its armed forces were equipped to deal with it. But maintaining and strengthening a military is a massive expense. Countries need to spend on hiring, training and retaining personnel, building and maintaining military infrastructure, and acquiring crucial technology such as tanks, fighter jets, warships, carriers and interceptors to power their defence. A well-trained, technologically advanced military is a huge asset for any country, allowing it to exert greater power over its opponents.

At the time of Independence, India lacked the technological know-how necessary for military modernization and needed extensive foreign assistance. But weighed down by scarce foreign exchange and enormous social and economic needs, the government was reluctant to spend too much on military development. Instead, it wanted to focus on industrial development and felt that defence would also benefit from this. In 1956, while addressing the Parliament, Prime Minister Jawaharlal Nehru said:

> 'Defence does not consist in people . . . marching up and down the road with guns and other weapons. Defence consists today in a country being industrially prepared for producing the goods and equipment of defence.'

While India did purchase some new technology, such as fighter jets, transport aircraft and tanks, it also attempted to make do with what was available and build indigenous technology. Local ordnance factories—the oldest arms manufacturers in India—mainly produced rifles based on British technology. A few years before Independence, the Indian industrialist Seth Walchand Hirachand had set up Hindustan Aircraft Limited, now Hindustan Aeronautics Limited (HAL), which assembled foreign aircraft in India under a license. In 1947, HAL was roped in to refurbish foreign military aircraft that had been abandoned in India after World War II to meet the needs of the Indian armed forces. HAL was also called upon to tinker with foreign purchases in order to make them more suitable for local needs. For example, it retrofitted the C-119 American cargo planes acquired in the 1950s with turbojet engines that allowed them to operate better in the high Himalayas. In 1956, HAL embarked on one of independent India's most ambitious defence projects of the time—designing and producing a fighter jet. Unfortunately, the jet—HF-24 Marut—was beset by engine troubles and failed to live up to expectations.

**Make a Trip**

Interested in exploring HAL's contributions to air defence and space technology in India? Visit the company's Heritage Centre and Aerospace Museum in Bengaluru.

Even as the military struggled with ageing technology and homegrown equipment, the government continued to believe that this was the right way to go. This attitude, though, was thoroughly demolished by a devastating turn of events in 1962.

## A Taste of Defeat

The raging border dispute over Kashmir had haunted Indo-Pak relations from the outset of Independence, and India didn't want any trouble with its other neighbours. But this is precisely what happened in the 1950s when China annexed Tibet, along India's north-eastern border, and then claimed large parts of Ladakh and Arunachal Pradesh as its territory. Unwilling to accept the possibility of war, the government tried its best to resolve the dispute diplomatically.

Violent border clashes in August and October 1959 prompted India to begin setting up small posts along its border with China. However, no definitive steps were taken to prepare the army. Tensions worsened in November 1959 when India granted asylum to the Dalai Lama—Tibet's spiritual leader and head of state. Despite such developments, Nehru and his defence minister, V.K. Krishna Menon, continued to believe that the dispute with China could be resolved without war.

Between 19 and 20 October 1962, war broke out. Wave upon wave of Chinese troops stormed into India under the cover of blazing firepower. The Chinese outnumbered and overwhelmed India's defences. In occupying Tibet, they had fought off Tibetan rebels in the inhospitable Himalayan region and, unlike the Indian troops, were used to warfare in the high mountains. Troop movement was also easier—they had already built infrastructure on their end and only needed to descend into India. Indian troops, on the other hand, needed to climb up steep slopes with no proper roads and frequent mudslides to reach the border. Trucks broke down or got stuck and had to be dragged by groups of soldiers. Some parts of the Himalayan region could only be accessed on mules. Although the air force was used for troop movement and dropping supplies, it wasn't engaged extensively in the battles.

Poor planning and the lack of defence spending proved to be extremely detrimental to India. Let alone artillery, many of its troops didn't even have enough necessary clothing, such as coats and gloves, to protect them from the harsh weather. Despite the valour of Indian soldiers, the Chinese overran Indian defences with remarkable ease. About a month into the war, a distraught Nehru dispatched secret letters to US

President John F. Kennedy, including one requesting radar stations and twelve squadrons of all-weather fighter jets. Since the Indian military did not have the training to operate such technology at the time, American personnel were requested for this.

This was an astonishing request that flew in the face of India's decision to not align with any superpower. But before Kennedy got around to replying to Nehru's letters, the Chinese declared a unilateral ceasefire on 21 November and withdrew to the positions they had held before 20 October. Why had the Chinese withdrawn so suddenly? Some believed that this was because all political parties in India, including the communists, were firmly supporting the Indian government. Others felt that supplies of Western arms had deterred the Chinese. Another important consideration was the change in season. Winter was setting in, and soon the Himalayas would be covered in snow, making it difficult for China to send supplies to its troops fighting on Indian plains.

Following the Chinese withdrawal, India regained most of its lost territory. But the war had left it deeply humiliated. Its dreams of being a non-violent force had been crushed by the trauma of defeat. Building military might was the need of the hour. Defence could neither rely on ageing technology nor wait for India to become capable of designing and manufacturing its own military technology.

Electronic equipment had been found to be embarrassingly lacking, and in the aftermath of the 1962 war, the government gave a determined push to electronics manufacturing in India (*also see page 90*). The Air Defence Ground Environment System to detect and intercept aerial incursions into India's airspace, for example, was developed during the 1970s on a Trombay Digital Computer

(TDC), the first indigenously manufactured computer. Similarly, in 1977, the army collaborated with the Tata Institute of Fundamental Research to develop software for the Army Radio Engineering Network. Although slow-moving, these early initiatives laid the foundation for the electronic capabilities of the Indian armed forces. The Signal Corps, who handle the communication network of the Indian army, for instance, have some of the world's most capable coders.

Even though India began spending more money on its military to make it bigger and better, the Cold War between the US and the Soviet Union (now Russia), and India's decision to avoid aligning with either side, frequently got in the way.

## Russian Roulette

At the time of Independence, most of India's military technology was British. Most of its imports, soon after Independence, were also from US-led Western countries. But technological support from these countries hit a roadblock in 1955 when Pakistan decided to align with the US and acquired military assistance from it, in return for allowing the US to use its ports and airbases. Although some equipment from the West still made its way to India, the military had to increasingly look elsewhere for technological support.

By the 1960s, military assistance from the Soviet Union began to grow. The Soviet-made MiG 21 was one of the best combat aircraft of its time, and in 1962, India decided to acquire it. The first six MiG 21s arrived in India in 1963 and formed a new IAF squadron. More helpfully, the Soviets had licensed the technology to India, allowing the rest of the aircraft to be manufactured locally. To further ease matters, they had agreed to let India pay for much of the deal in Indian rupees, saving scarce foreign exchange. This was a truly generous offer because the Soviet Union could only use the rupees to buy goods from India.

MiG 21

The MiG 21 deal marked the beginning of the Indian military's gradual shift to Soviet technology, which continues to have a prominent presence even today. Back in the day, this sent the West into a tizzy as it appeared to confirm fears that despite its apparent non-alignment, India was aligning with the Soviet Union. Various strategies were used to counter the development. The US and Britain offered to supply India with some British fighter jets and American carriers if it backed out of the MiG deal. However, this was a limited offer with no provision for local manufacture, and India declined.

Another proposal was made to help India resolve the engine troubles of the indigenous HF-24 Marut fighter jet. However, the suggested engines were still under development, and India was unwilling to bet on unrealized designs. This proposal, too, fell through. By this time, the Indian government made it clear that it had no intention of abandoning the MiG 21 deal, and this ended the negotiations with the American bloc.

In January 1965, the Indian government expressed an interest in acquiring the Northrop F-5A Freedom Fighters, supersonic fighter planes that the US was willing to offer. India had initially declined this offer, wanting to hold out for the superior Lockheed F-104G Starfighter. When this did not materialize, it agreed to acquire the F-5As to replace some of its ageing Western aircraft that were becoming expensive to maintain. However, this deal failed when yet another Indo-Pak war broke out, and the US government decided not to fulfil India's request.

The 1965 war showcased the military might Pakistan had accumulated during the 1950s with American assistance. Its armour now boasted of several technologically advanced instruments of war, including the M48 Patton tanks, M24 Chaffee tanks, the Lockheed F-104G Starfighter, the F-86 Sabre jet fighter, the C-130 Hercules transport aircraft and an army equipped with the Belgian-made 7.62mm Self-loading Rifle (SLR). On the other hand, India's armed forces had just begun the process of modernization and had to largely rely on ageing technology. Yet, what they lacked in technological prowess, they tried to make up with strategy and greater field experience with existing technology. In the end, both countries suffered heavily in the conflict and a ceasefire was negotiated by the Soviet Union at Tashkent in January 1966.

For India, the war was further proof of the grim military challenges before it. It had suffered a heavy loss against China in 1962. Meanwhile, Pakistan had emerged as a formidable opponent with a modernized military. Growing cooperation between China and Pakistan only made matters worse, as it raised the possibility of a joint Sino-Pak strike.

## A Thumping Victory

Partition had split Pakistan into two halves—one in the east and the other in the west, separated by thousands of kilometres of Indian territory. Culturally, the two halves were very different from each other, with mostly Bengali-speaking people in the east and Urdu-speaking people in the west. East Pakistan felt neglected by the leadership in West Pakistan. Even resources were divided unequally between the two halves, and the east was poorer than the west. However, it had a much larger population and in 1970, following Pakistan's first election, the Awami League, led by the Bengali-Muslim leader Sheikh Mujibur Rehman, swept to power by winning an absolute majority of 160 seats—all of which were in the east. This was unacceptable to the leadership in the west. General Yahya Khan, the President of Pakistan, responded by imposing martial law in the east, imprisoning Rehman and appointing General Tikka Khan as the leader of East Pakistan. Thereafter, the Pakistani army began a systematic crackdown—Operation Searchlight—on the Bengali population. Lakhs of Bengalis, regardless of their religion, were killed, leading to a mass exodus and an intense refugee crisis along India's border with East Pakistan.

The Mukti Bahini—a guerrilla force of Bengali officers and soldiers who had defected from East Pakistan's army, as well as independent volunteers—took refuge in India. They started training camps and began launching attacks against the forces occupying their homeland. West Pakistan accused India of instigating the defectors, and in December 1971, another Indo-Pak war broke out.

A few months before the war, India had signed a Treaty of Friendship and Cooperation with the Soviet Union, which opened the floodgates for Soviet military equipment licensed for production to India. Additional MiG 21s fitted with extra firepower were quickly produced, along with a few Sukhoi-7 fighter jets to boost India's air attack. Hardy Mi helicopters were also acquired. The Indian army was supplemented with a large number of Russian guns and tanks. The 1971 war also saw the debut of the Vijayanta tank—India's first indigenous main battle tank—which was based on a technology transfer from the British engineering company Vickers-Armstrong. On full fuel, the tank could travel 530 kilometres. It could fire at enemy positions even at night and create a smoke screen to shield itself from enemy eyes.

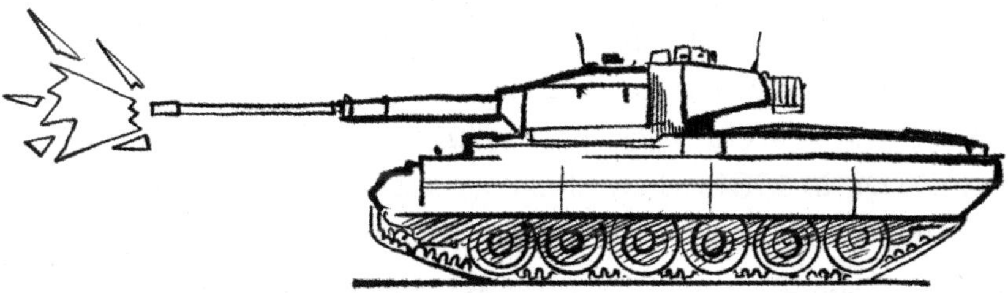

Vijayanta tank

The 1971 war was the first in which the navy played a defining role. At the centre of its efforts was INS *Vikrant*—India's first aircraft carrier—armed with combat aircraft, helicopters, missile-equipped warships and submarines.

Realizing its significance, Pakistan had secretly deployed a powerful US-made submarine—PNS *Ghazi*—to destroy the carrier a few weeks before the war. But it was intercepted and thwarted by the Indian navy. In the war that commenced shortly afterwards, INS *Vikrant* was able to successfully cut off Pakistan's communication lines in the Bay of Bengal and add to India's aerial strength.

Even though its military modernization was far from complete, India secured a thumping victory in the 1971 war that led to East Pakistan becoming Bangladesh. A few years later, India added yet another milestone in its growing military might.

## Smiling Buddha

The inconceivable destruction caused by the nuclear bombs dropped on Japan during World War II had pushed the world into a nuclear age where most countries coveted nuclear weapons to defend themselves. Newly independent India also spent large amounts of money on nuclear energy, but in keeping with its non-violent tradition, its leaders chose to pursue peaceful uses, particularly electricity generation. However, in 1964, when China successfully tested a nuclear weapon and became a nuclear-weapon state, India felt worried about its security. Although it approached the other nuclear-weapon states requesting their protection if it was threatened by China, it failed to get adequate assurance.

By the end of the 1960s, a group of scientists and researchers at the Bhabha Atomic Research Centre in Mumbai began serious work on developing nuclear weapons. After a series of struggles, doubts and worries, on the morning of 18 May 1974, they tested India's first nuclear bomb at Pokhran in Rajasthan. Nuclear physicist Raja Ramanna, who led the team, conveyed the successful testing to Prime Minister Indira Gandhi with a coded message, 'The Buddha is smiling.' That's how the test—Pokhran I—came to be called Operation Smiling Buddha.

The government declared that the test was a peaceful nuclear explosion and that India was not a nuclear-weapon state. But most countries refused to believe this. In 1975, a group of countries got together to form the Nuclear Suppliers Group, which stopped the export of nuclear technology and fuel to India. This was a major setback for India's nuclear programme that still needed international technological assistance. In the absence of such help, technological development was delayed by a few decades. Meanwhile, alarmed by the test, neighbouring Pakistan initiated its own nuclear weapons programme.

## Nuclear Energy

All chemical elements are made up of atoms. Inside every atom is a nucleus that holds enormous amounts of energy. In most atoms, this energy remains locked within the nucleus. However, some chemical elements, such as uranium and plutonium, can release this nuclear energy in the form of powerful radiation. These elements are known as radioactive elements.

In the late 1930s, scientists in Germany discovered that atoms of radioactive elements could be split apart to release nuclear energy. This splitting is called nuclear fission. During the 1940s, scientists in the US developed a nuclear reactor—a device to initiate, sustain and control nuclear fission. This was a significant scientific breakthrough, as it made it possible to harness nuclear energy. Even though reactor technology was first used to make nuclear bombs, soon afterwards, it was tapped to produce electricity. During the 1950s, with Western assistance, India built its first nuclear reactor called Apsara and also acquired a reactor from Canada called CIRUS (Canada-India Reactor, US). By the 1960s, India had set up its first nuclear power plant at Tarapur, near Mumbai. Eventually, though, reactor technology was also used to produce India's first nuclear bomb.

## Missile Programme

When India conducted its first nuclear test, it possessed just a few crude bombs that could be dropped on enemy positions by certain kinds of fighter jets. What India needed was missiles mounted with nuclear warheads that could travel long distances over land, air and water to strike enemy targets. Although it had acquired some missiles from Russia, these were not adequate. So, in the 1970s, India's Defence Research and Development Organisation (DRDO) initiated a project, code-named Project Devil, to upgrade the country's missile technology.

The project began by re-engineering the Russian missiles to understand the technology before attempting to develop it indigenously. A parallel programme—Project Valiant—was also initiated to build a more powerful, liquid-propelled missile engine. In addition to these two projects, the DRDO also began to create a guidance or navigation system to direct missiles over long distances and ensure that they hit their targets accurately. By developing indigenous potential, the scientists at DRDO wanted to reduce India's excessive dependence on foreign technology.

In the early 1980s, all these projects were combined into the Integrated Guided Missile Development Programme. It was headed by A.P.J. Abdul Kalam, who had been working on India's space programme and had helped develop its first rocket—the Satellite Launch Vehicle (SLV).

### All About Missiles

A missile is a weapon that can travel at great speeds and strike targets with an explosive warhead.

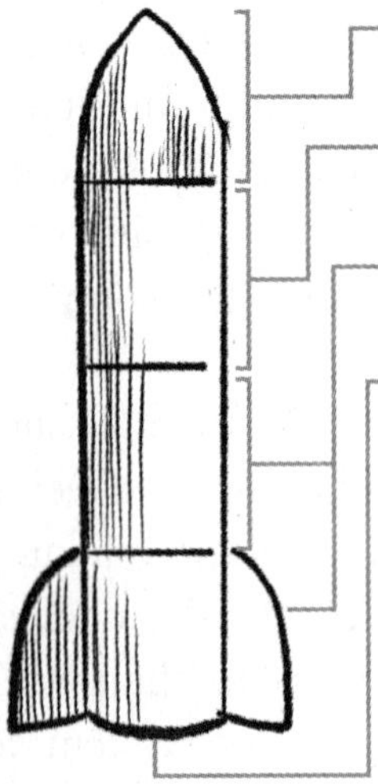

- **The warhead** is the explosive carried by a missile.
- **The guidance system** guides a missile in the correct direction.
- **The control system** commands the movement of the missile.
- **The engine** generates the force required to propel a missile (propulsion). It is powered by fuel, which is usually either solid or liquid. Sometimes, a mix of two fuels or a hybrid is also used. Rockets can also be propelled by engines that use atmospheric oxygen instead of oxygen from an inbuilt oxidizer to burn fuel.

## Types of missiles

- **Based on trajectory** (the path they follow after they are launched):

• Ballistic missiles arc high up, outside the atmosphere, and then descend to hit their target
• Cruise missiles remain within the atmosphere with a near constant height and speed

Ballistic and cruise missiles can be further categorized based on their range, speed and method of launching.

- **Based on range** (the distance they can travel):

1. Short range: Travel less than 1,000 kms
2. Medium range: Travel between 1,000 and 3,000 kms

3. Intermediate: Travel between 3,000 and 5,500 kms
4. Intercontinental: Travel over 5,500 kms

**Based on speed:**

1. Subsonic: Travel slower than the speed of sound
2. Supersonic: Travel faster than the speed of sound
3. Hypersonic: Travel at least five times faster than the speed of sound

**Based on the method of launching:**

**Air-to-Air Missiles:** Launched from an aircraft towards another.

**Surface-to-Air Missiles:** Launched from land-based platforms to strike aerial targets, such as aircraft and drones.

**Air-to-Surface Missiles:** Launched from an aircraft towards ground-based targets.

**Surface-to-Surface Missiles:** Launched from land-based platforms to strike ground targets. Also includes missiles that are launched by a ship or submarine towards another ship or submarine.

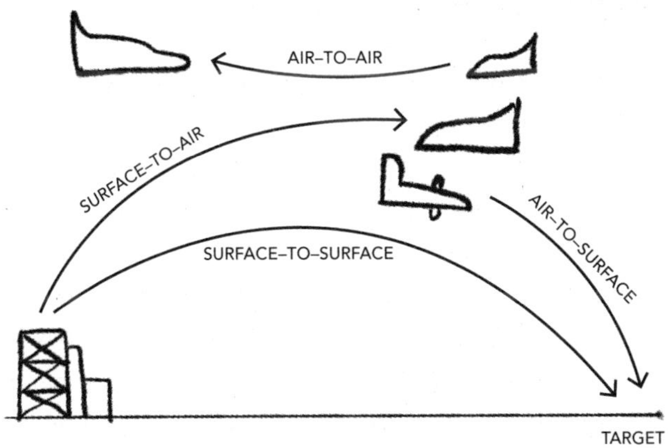

Under Kalam's supervision, the DRDO successfully tested Prithvi-I, India's first missile, in 1988. It could travel up to 150 kilometres and carry a warhead weighing 1,000 kilograms. The following year, DRDO tested Agni-I, which could travel a longer distance. Shortly after the Agni test, the Missile Technology Control Regime—an informal group of US-led Western countries that sought to control the spread of missile technology—decided to impose restrictions on exporting critical components required by India's missile programme. Like the Nuclear Suppliers Group, this was another restraint placed on India's military development.

In the face of this setback, the DRDO created a consortium of laboratories, public sector companies and academic institutions to make a joint effort to produce what was needed, and bit by bit, the results began to show. For example, the magnesium alloy that India had been importing from Germany for the Prithvi missile began to roll out of the public sector company Mishra Dhatu Nigam Limited (MIDHANI) in Hyderabad.

## Becoming a Nuclear-Weapon State

By the 1990s, the DRDO had made significant strides in developing India's missile programme. Neighbouring Pakistan, too, was working on a similar programme, which prevented India from succumbing to the enormous international pressure against its missile programme. For instance, the Agni programme, which was briefly put on hold in 1995–1996 following international pressure, was revived in 1997 when Pakistan tested the Ghaznavi missile, which was capable of striking targets in India with a 700-kilogram warhead.

On 6 April 1998, Pakistan tested the Ghauri missile that could travel close to 1,500 kilometres, striking major cities deep inside India. Deeply troubled by this development, India decided to take a bold step. The very next month, on 11 May, it detonated three nuclear bombs and declared itself a nuclear-weapon state. Two days later, on 13 May, it detonated two more nuclear bombs. The top-secret tests came as a shock to the world and prompted neighbouring Pakistan to test its own bombs towards the end of May. A year later, India successfully tested the Agni-II missile, which could travel up to 2,000 kilometres and carry a warhead weighing 1,000 kilograms. Although these developments invited harsh international criticism and more sanctions against India's military modernization, they were a major milestone in its ability to defend itself.

In 2008, India concluded the Integrated Guided Missile Development Programme, even though it continued making missiles. The programme had led to the development of various missiles, significantly boosting India's missile-making ability. Kalam, who headed the programme, came to be known as the Missile Man of India. The same year, India also closed the Indo-US Civil Nuclear Deal that lifted the barriers imposed on it by the Nuclear Suppliers Group. In exchange, India allowed the International Atomic Energy Association (IAEA) to inspect its nuclear programme to ensure the peaceful use of nuclear technology and fuel. India was also expected to follow international safeguards on disarmament and non-proliferation and continue its voluntary halt on further nuclear testing.

The civil nuclear deal allowed India to participate in the international nuclear community and join groups like the Missile Technology Control Regime, giving it greater access to critical technologies. In 2018, India finally gained the ability to launch nuclear strikes not just on land and air but also underwater, when it successfully launched the Sagarika missile from the first indigenous nuclear submarine INS *Arihant*. Called a nuclear-triad, this three-sided nuclear strike ability was another major milestone in India's military technology.

### The Missile Woman

In the highly secretive, male-dominated world of missile development, Tessy Thomas from the DRDO is a shining example of a woman scientist working on strategic nuclear ballistic missiles. She was the first woman to lead missile teams in India and is fondly called the country's Missile Woman.

## Weaponizing Space

Although India's space programme (*also see page 49*) had been founded under the Atomic Energy Commission, binding it to the atomic (nuclear) programme, it was primarily interested in projects leading to social and economic development. But as India's defence needs became more urgent, military objectives creeped in.

One of the most controversial creations of space programmes are intelligence-gathering or spy satellites. Orbiting Earth, these satellites can survey pre-selected areas to transmit extremely detailed images of what is happening on the ground. Such information can leak a country's top-secret missions to its opponents, posing a major security risk. In 1995, for example, US intelligence-gathering satellites surveying Pokhran had spotted what appeared to be preparations for a nuclear test. This put India under tremendous pressure, and it had to cancel the test. Having learnt this lesson, the team behind the 1998 nuclear tests prepared an elaborate plan to evade satellite surveillance. They dressed up as army men instead of bomb builders and testers and worked in the open desert only when they knew the spy satellites were not overhead. That's how the mission remained top secret till the very end!

In 1999, militants backed by the Pakistani army made a surprising and audacious attempt to capture the high mountains overlooking the strategic Srinagar-Kargil-Leh National Highway connecting Kashmir and Ladakh. This led to a war in which the Indian army and air force would have benefitted from satellite images of the enemy build-up. But the Indian space programme did not possess such technology at the time. The US had satellites which could have provided the images requested by the Indian military, but given its ties to Pakistan, it did not agree to the request. At the end of the war, space-based surveillance was recognized as a major technological requirement and the space programme began working on the Technology Experiment Satellite (TES). It was designed and built in just two years—by 2001 India had the ability to get high-resolution satellite images for military purposes.

Another space-based military threat to India emerged in 2007 when China tested a ballistic missile that could destroy satellites in space. The ability to destroy a satellite orbiting in space is an enormous technological feat because it involves targeting a fast-moving object with a moving weapon. The chances of error are very high. Yet, in 2019, India became the fourth nation, after the US, Russia and China, to possess an anti-satellite (ASAT) missile.

## Moving Towards Self-Reliance

Since Independence, India had harboured dreams of becoming self-reliant in all aspects, including defence. Even though various attempts were made to accomplish this, insufficient technological know-how came in the way, and India continued to rely on foreign countries for defence technology. In 1991, the Soviet Union, India's largest defence supplier, disintegrated to form several independent countries—the largest of which was Russia. This added to India's problems because replacing and maintaining the military technologies acquired from the Soviets became harder. However, by the end of the 1990s, buoyed by the success of its nuclear and missile programmes, India gained greater confidence in its ability to support itself. It now aimed to meet 70 per cent of its military requirements on its own.

Before it could do this, India needed to arm its military with a range of equipment that would, at the very least, match, if not surpass, those of its main adversaries. It also needed to possess the ability to maintain the operational effectiveness of its equipment and obtain spares and other support under all conditions. To do this, India began forging defence-related ties with more countries, such as France, and gradually permitted private companies into its defence industry, allowing them to play a greater role in manufacturing defence equipment for the country. India also increased military exercises with other nations to give its armed forces greater exposure and experience and contributed troops to UN peacekeeping missions.

In January 2011, the Indian ministry of defence came up with its first ever Defence Production Policy to improve self-reliance. A decade later, the government began issuing lists of various defence components and subsystems that could not be imported but had to be bought from Indian firms. In 2023, these lists contained more than 3,000 items.

Over the years, India has also inducted many indigenously designed and built technologies into its armed forces. One of its major successes is the LCA Tejas, a light combat aircraft manufactured by HAL, that was inducted into the armed forces in 2015.

The 2023 Republic Day parade was a grand spectacle of India's indigenous accomplishments in defence. For the first time, the customary twenty-one-gun salute was made using 105-mm field guns manufactured in India. Other made-in-India equipment on display included the K-9 Vajra-T gun system, BMP-2/2K Infantry Combat Vehicles, Arjun Main Battle Tank, the Nag and the BrahMos Missile and the Akash air defence missile system. However, it is important to note that even though many technologies are labelled indigenous, not every component and system powering them is made in India. Many are still imported from overseas, while some have been made with active international collaboration, such as the BrahMos Missile that has been developed jointly with Russia.

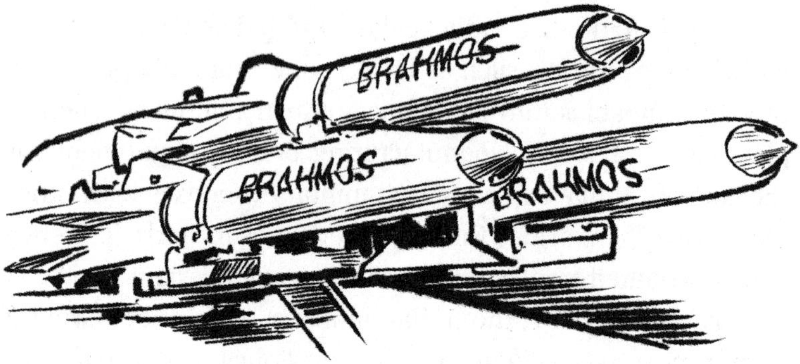


Apart from improving self-reliance, India has also gradually been increasing its defence exports—something which was inconceivable at the time of Independence and for several decades thereafter. Although most of India's exports have been to other countries in Asia and the Middle East, its earnings from these exports has grown over the years, crossing a record 21,000 crores in 2023–2024. India's biggest export deal so far has been the sale of a version of the BrahMos cruise missile, which was delivered to the Philippines in April 2024.

## An Uncertain Future

Although India has made giant strides in boosting military technology since Independence, a lot remains to be done. According to the Stockholm International Peace Research Institute, even though India's arms imports have dropped between 2013 and 2022, it remains one of the world's largest defence importers.

Allegations of bribes paid to secure defence contracts have marred many of its imports—Bofors gun, AugustaWestland helicopter, Rafale fighter aircraft—creating much ill-will and slowing down purchases.

The quality of India's military armour has also been questioned on several occasions because of accidents and mishaps. The MiG 21, for example, came to be infamously known as the Flying Coffin during the 1990s after a series of accidents that claimed the lives of hundreds of pilots. Preventing such incidents through adequate maintenance is essential to improve self-reliance.

Finally, in a changing world, the nature of warfare has also changed. Technological advancements have led to an increase in non-contact warfare, where countries fight each other from a distance, using weapons such as missiles and drones. An even more insidious form of non-contact war is one which avoids weapons and instead uses technology to target a country's computer systems, its economy and even the minds of its people! Such attacks can include hacking into high-security computer networks, blocking trade and spreading misinformation through social media to divide or mislead people on sensitive issues. Over the years, India has made several strides in handling all kinds of non-contact warfare. In 2019, for instance, it established the Defence Cyber Agency to defend its military systems against cyberattacks.

Born in the aftermath of the devastating World War II, independent India has continued to live with violence for decades. While military technology is not an answer to violence, it is essential for defence in a violent world. In the years since Independence, India has made significant progress in developing modern military technology. Although there is always room for improvement, it is certainly better armed than ever before to face the uncertain future.

# 3

# Reaching for the Stars

On 4 October 1957, a beeping sound could be heard on radios around the world. It came from Sputnik I—a satellite that the Soviet Union (now Russia) had launched into space. In the midst of the Cold War between the Soviets and the Americans, this technological feat of the Soviet Union kicked off an epic Space Race between the two superpowers. The US established the National Aeronautics and Space Administration (NASA) and immediately began working on a space programme of its own. In 1961, the Russian astronaut Yuri Gagarin became the first human to travel to space. Not to be outdone, in 1962, US President John F. Kennedy boldly proclaimed that before the end of the decade NASA would land a man on the Moon and return him safely to Earth.

Away from this high-stakes rivalry, another man, Indian scientist and industrialist Vikram Ambalal Sarabhai, was dreaming of taking his country into space. But his dream seemed impossible because India was a country with meagre means, endless needs and no space scientists or infrastructure.

## A Nation Begins to Dream

Space programmes are enormously expensive and technologically complex. So, in 1961 when Sarabhai proposed such a programme for India, it would have been easy to laugh off his outrageous proposal. But Prime Minister Jawaharlal Nehru was convinced that science and technology held the key to improving the quality of human life, and he didn't want India to fall behind in the Space Age. Homi Bhabha, one of India's most influential scientists, who was heading the country's nuclear programme, also agreed that the India needed to pursue space research.

In the complete absence of necessary experience and infrastructure, foreign help was vital. So, in February 1962, India established the Indian National Committee for Space Research (INCOSPAR) with sponsorship from the United Nations (UN) and appointed Sarabhai to lead it.

INCOSPAR's first mission was to launch a sounding rocket that would travel about 100 kilometres above Earth to study a powerful electric current called the equatorial electrojet (EEJ) flowing in the atmosphere. With the UN's backing, the mission was able to acquire much-needed technological assistance from abroad: the US would supply its efficient and reliable Nike-Apache sounding rocket, France would provide a sodium vapour cylinder to be placed inside the rocket and the Soviet Union would supply a computer to monitor the mission.

Setting up a team of scientists and engineers for the project was also an international endeavour. Sarabhai not only recruited Indian scientists and engineers working overseas but also sent local scientists and engineers to international space centres to gain knowledge in space research.

Rocket launches are a risky undertaking because rockets take off with a powerful blast, and sometimes, instead of shooting up, they unexpectedly change direction. That's why launch sites are typically located in remote, thinly populated coastal areas, where the chances of accidents causing massive damage are fewer. With a coastline of over 11,000 kilometres, India had plenty of options open to it. In the end, the team chose Thumba, a 2.5-kilometre-long fishing hamlet in Kerala, squeezed between a railway station and the Arabian Sea, for India's first rocket launch. The EEJ flowed directly above it, making it a good spot to collect data on the current.

The largest building in Thumba was the church of St Mary Magdalene. It was at the heart of the local fishing community. INCOSPAR sought permission to use the church to set up the Thumba Equatorial Rocket Launching Station (TERLS)—and got it in record time too! Despite the inconvenience it caused them, the people of Thumba generously made room for this grand enterprise. Many of them had to move to another village nearby. Meanwhile, their church, the bishop's house and cattle sheds were turned into workshops, offices, storage rooms and laboratories of India's first space centre.

The facilities at Thumba were scant. In the absence of other suitable transport, bicycles and bullock carts were used to transport rocket parts. Many young scientists on the small team had little experience in space research. But what they lacked in facilities and experience, they made up for with determination and enthusiasm, as they began assembling their very first rocket. This, though, was not an easy task.

Transporting the American rocket and French cylinder safely to Thumba was a challenge in itself. But once they arrived, it was found that the cylinder did not fit inside the rocket because the US and France had used different systems of measurement! The cylinder had to be reduced in size for it to fit inside the rocket. This needed to be done with extreme caution because of the explosive sodium vapour in the cylinder. Ratilal Panchal, a skilled mechanic from the Physical Research Laboratory in Ahmedabad, was summoned to manually reduce the size of the cylinder as two scientists from the team sat with him.

Launch at Thumba

On 21 November 1963, India was ready for its first rocket launch. But the crane that was going to lift the assembled rocket malfunctioned and the team had to do the lifting manually. Five minutes before the launch, a loud alarm was sounded, instructing everyone to clear the site. Despite this, a man was found still adjusting the launcher and had to be hurriedly evacuated.

Finally, at 6.23 p.m., two minutes after sunset, the rocket was launched. Minutes later, it reached its maximum altitude and an orange glow from the exploding sodium vapour illuminated the twilight. It formed a column in the sky that the scientists monitored using radar, camera and visual observations to study the EEJ.

India's entry into the Space Age was a triumph. In the midst of the bitter Cold War, Thumba—a UN-sponsored facility in a non-aligned nation—became a place for friendly collaboration between scientists from different countries. For several years, it continued launching sounding rockets for various countries.

On 15 August 1969, INCOSPAR became the Indian Space Research Organisation (ISRO), marking the beginning of a historic journey for the country.

# Orbits and Satellites

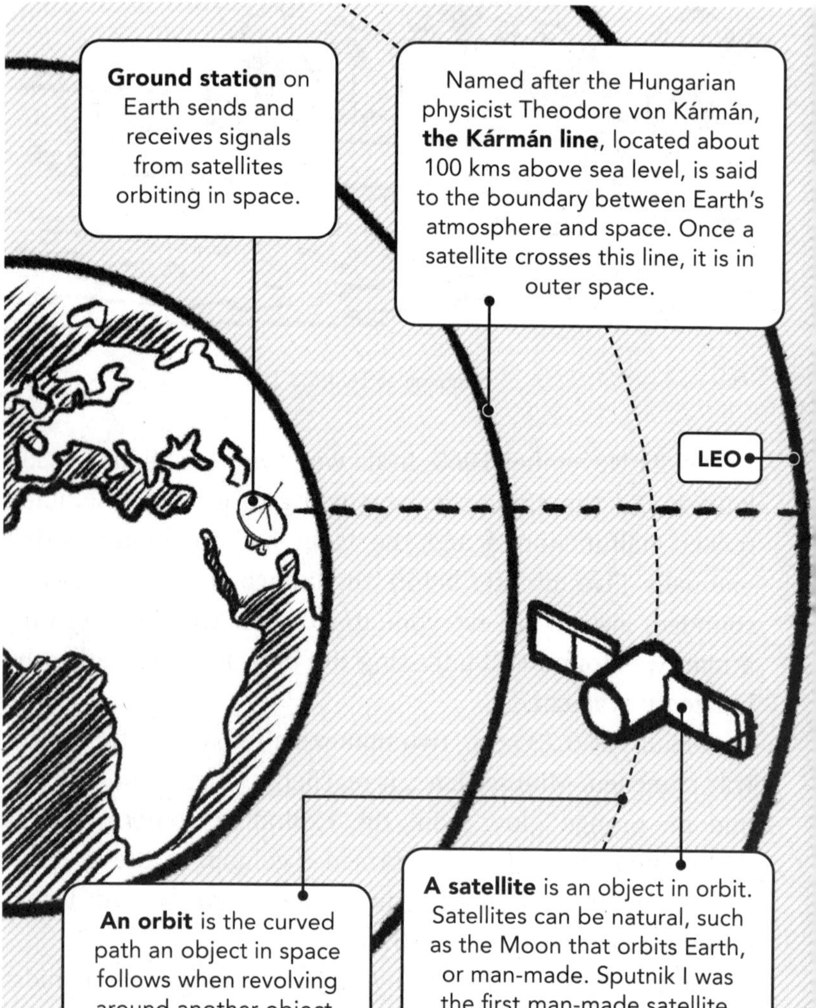


A satellite orbiting Earth is in constant tension with the pull of gravity. Without gravity, the satellite would go off into space once it's launched. The tension with gravity keeps the satellite orbiting around the planet, till it's finally pulled into Earth's atmosphere. Most satellites burn up on entering the atmosphere.

There are different types of satellite orbits. They can be classified as:

**Low Earth Orbit (LEO)**: 160 to 2,000 kilometres above Earth. This is the most popular orbit and includes satellites such as the Hubble Space Telescope and the International Space Station

**Medium Earth Orbit (MEO)**: 2,000 to less than 35,786 kilometres above Earth

**Geosynchronous Orbit (GEO)**: 35,786 kilometres above Earth

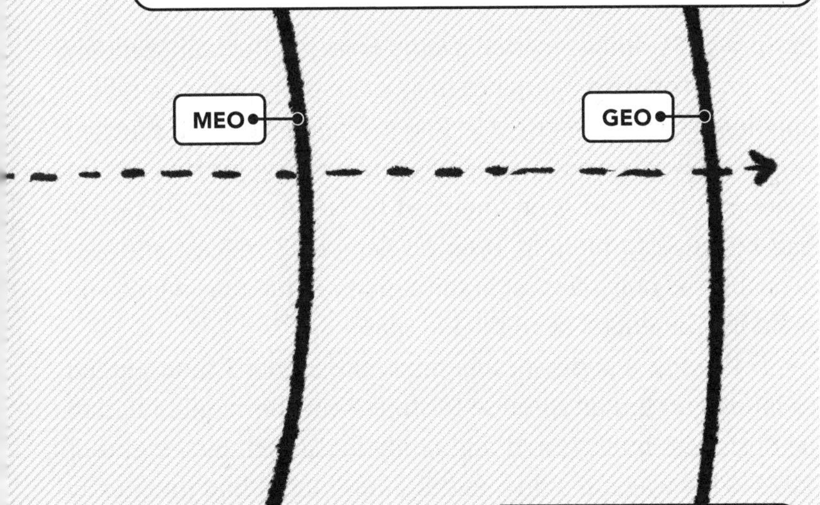

Satellites in **equatorial orbit** travel west to east.

Satellites in **polar orbit** travel from north to south, passing over the polar regions of the Earth.

**Make a Trip**

Interested in exploring the birthplace of the Indian Space Programme? Plan a trip to the Vikram Sarabhai Space Centre's Space Museum at Thumba.

## The First Satellite

In April 1971, India received a letter from the Russian Academy of Sciences offering assistance to its space programme. Sarabhai appointed space scientist U.R. Rao to lead this project. Rao had been closely involved in designing and building instruments for spacecraft that had been launched by NASA in the 1960s. He had returned to India in 1966 on Sarabhai's request and was probably the only scientist in the country at the time who could build instruments that worked in space.

Following a series of meetings, the Soviet Union agreed to launch an Indian satellite for free—but the satellite had to be designed, built, tested and ready for launch by the end of 1974. This was a massive undertaking. India had practically no knowledge of how to build a satellite, there were no experienced personnel or space-related industries and no infrastructure to support such an endeavour. Some scientists thought this was an impossible feat and wanted India to pass up the offer. But Rao was convinced that this was a great opportunity for the country to acquire the technological know-how required to build its space programme.

In the midst of these deliberations came a shocking news—Sarabhai had died in his sleep on 30 December 1971. His sudden death fuelled a searing ambition in India's budding space programme to fulfil his dreams. So, in mid-1972, ISRO began a momentous journey towards designing and building its first satellite. The clock was ticking and to save time, it was decided that the satellite would be built in Bangalore (now Bengaluru) instead of Thumba because most companies supplying electronics and other technical systems were based there. By September 1972, a makeshift facility came up in an industrial estate in Bangalore, which eventually became the state-of-the-art ISRO Satellite Centre (now the UR Rao Satellite Centre).

The small team of scientists and engineers, most of whom had never seen a satellite before, worked round the clock to build one. The satellite was a twenty-six-sided polyhedron with solar panels covering all its sides except the top and bottom. It carried three instruments that would study sunrays, as well as conditions in the ionosphere (where the atmosphere meets space). Specialized equipment and components unavailable in India were speedily acquired from the US, UK and France. Prime Minister Indira Gandhi chose to call the satellite Aryabhata after the ancient Indian mathematician and astronomer.

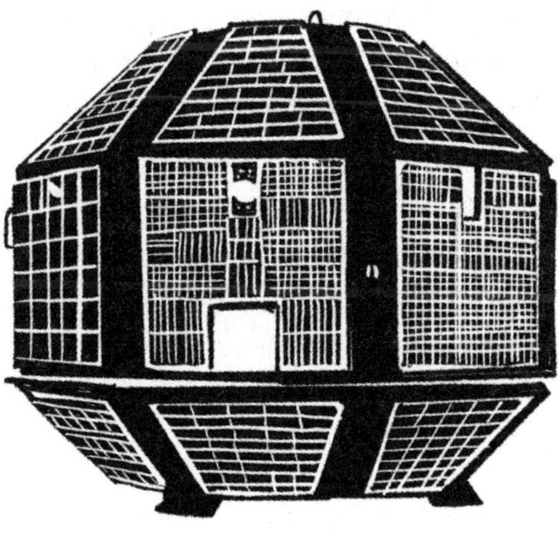

Aryabhata

The space centre at Sriharikota in Andhra Pradesh, which had been operational since October 1971, was chosen as the primary ground station for communicating with the satellite, but a backup was needed. So, two months before the launch, two toilets at the makeshift facility in Bangalore were converted into an operational ground station! Finally, everything was in place. With rudimentary facilities and a shoestring budget, a small team of novice engineers had built a satellite in thirty-one months!

On 19 April 1975, Aryabhata was launched into space from a remote location in the Soviet Union. Thirty minutes into the launch, the first signals were detected at Sriharikota in India. Even though it eventually developed a fault in its power supply and could not carry out many experiments, Aryabhata did return some data and survived well past the target of six months in space. Most of all, it gave India's space programme the confidence that it, too, could design, build and operate a satellite in space. Rao, who led the project, came to be called the Satellite Man of India.

Two days after the launch of Aryabhata, ISRO signed an agreement with the Soviet Union to launch another satellite—Bhaskara 1. Named after yet another ancient Indian mathematician and astronomer, Bhaskara 1 was India's first experimental Earth observation satellite. It was launched on 7 June 1979. Eleven months after the launch, it sent back the first images of India from space. Even as ISRO took major strides in developing satellites, another milestone remained to be achieved to realize Sarabhai's dreams—rockets.

In 1977, NASA's *Voyager I* spacecraft was launched into space with a twelve-inch gold-plated copper disc. Known as the Voyager Golden Record, the disc contained musical compositions from around the world, reflecting Earth's diverse life and culture to any extra-terrestrial life forms that might encounter it. One of these compositions was Indian classical singer Kesarbai Kerkar's song 'Jaat Kahan Ho Akeli, Gori' (meaning, 'where are you going alone, girl'), making Kerkar the first Indian voice in outer space.

## Rockets vs Sounding Rockets

Rockets are powerful launch vehicles that are used to carry satellites and astronauts into space. Sounding rockets are less powerful and are mainly used to collect information on the atmosphere and space.

## Rocketing into Space

In 1969, as the US landed the first humans on the Moon, Sarabhai had been busy laying out his vision for India's space programme in the coming decade. By the end of the 1970s, he wanted India to be able to design, build and launch satellites into space. With Aryabhata, ISRO had proved its ability to design and build satellites. Now it needed to design and build rockets—launch vehicles that would carry its satellites into space.

Developing rockets had been ISRO's goal since the 1963 launch at Thumba. It had begun working towards this by building sounding rockets and producing rocket fuel. The first indigenous sounding rocket, Rohini 75, was launched from Thumba in November 1967. By the end of the 1960s, ISRO had also gained significant experience in producing solid fuel for rockets. It was now ready for the next step.

In the early 1970s, ISRO kicked off its first Satellite Launch Vehicle programme—SLV-3. Aerospace scientist A.P.J Abdul Kalam was appointed to lead it. The transition from making sounding rockets to making a launch vehicle was a formidable technological challenge. It became even more complex when satellites were heavier and had to be placed in higher orbits.

SLV-3 was designed to launch a 40-kilogram satellite into Low Earth Orbit (LEO). The design was broadly based on the hugely successful American Scout rockets. Around fifty industries and institutions outside ISRO were engaged in developing and building the major components and sub-systems for the SLV-3.

The first launch attempt in August 1979 failed. The scientists were disheartened as years of hard work and crores of rupees had been riding on the test. But despair would not do. So, they began again, and the very next year, on 18 July 1980, SLV-3 successfully placed the indigenous satellite Rohini-1 in space. With this, India became the sixth nation in the world to be able to design, build and launch its own satellites. The success of SLV-3 encouraged ISRO to begin developing more advanced rockets that could carry heavier satellites to higher orbits. Yet, it would take decades of trial and error, failure and success, before ISRO could finally come close to realizing Sarabhai's dream of self-sufficiency, with the Polar Satellite Launch Vehicle (PSLV).

## Towards Self-Sufficiency

After the success of the SLV-3, ISRO began working on the Augmented Satellite Launch Vehicle (ASLV). This was a heavier rocket, designed to carry a satellite weighing more than 100 kilograms to LEO. Although most ASLV flights did not go as planned, investigating the problems and finding solutions proved to be an invaluable experience and laid the foundation for the PSLV project in the 1990s.

So far, ISRO's rockets had relied on solid fuel. The biggest change in the PSLV was the introduction of liquid fuel. Not only is liquid fuel more efficient, rockets propelled by it are also easier to steer because the engine can be regulated, stopped and restarted multiple times in flight. This can offer greater thrust to the rocket, allowing it to go higher.

Liquid-fuel technology had come to India from France. During the 1970s, a team of ISRO scientists had helped France build its launch vehicle called Ariane on a tight budget and timeline. The Viking engine for Ariane was based on liquid-fuel technology. In return for the services rendered,

France transferred the technology to ISRO. The experience of working on Ariane and the technology transfer under this agreement led to the creation of VIKAS (derived from the initials of **Vik**ram **A**mbalal **S**arabhai)—India's first liquid-fuel engine that powered the PSLV.

After a failed attempt in September 1993, the PSLV was launched successfully in October 1994. Further launches boosted the rocket's performance, making it ISRO's more trusted launch vehicle. The PSLV can send satellites weighing around 1,400 kilograms to the Geosynchronous Orbit. It has been used to launch a majority of India's most important satellites, as well as the famous Chandrayaan and Mangalyaan missions that carried spacecraft to the Moon and to Mars.

## MOM on Mars

Launched on 5 November 2013, the Mars Orbiter Mission (MOM)—also called Mangalyaan—was ISRO's first interplanetary mission. It was an extremely complicated undertaking where timing was critical. MOM needed to complete a journey of 66,70,00,000 kilometres and reach a small fragment of space through which Mars would pass at 7.27 a.m. on 24 September 2014, as it orbited around the Sun. If MOM arrived earlier, it would crash into the red planet. If it was late, it would miss Mars and get lost in space. However, if it did manage to arrive at the right place at the right time, MOM would need to take one more critical step—slow down its speed to match the speed of Mars.

ISRO had never done this before, and previous missions by other countries had failed to meet the challenge on their first attempt.

On 24 September, India waited with bated breath for the first signals from MOM. After briefly disappearing behind Mars and losing contact with Earth, MOM sent its first signals to an Earth Station in Canberra, Australia, which forwarded them to ISRO, along with congratulations. India had become the first country in the world to reach Mars on its first attempt!

The success of the mission was captured in a flurry of national and international news and eventually in books, TV shows and films. Among other things, they hailed the significant number of women scientists on the project and its low cost. India had succeeded in completing the mission on a budget of approximately 450 crore rupees, whereas similar missions by countries like the US and Russia had cost thousands of crores.

Even though cost-effectiveness is impressive, it's worth considering whether celebrating this might be standing in ISRO's way of getting funding comparable to other premier space organizations in the world. After all, hasn't ISRO proved itself enough to merit funding that can compete with the best in the world?

During the 1990s, armed with the PSLV and the experience of having launched a variety of satellites, ISRO had made sufficient progress to tap into space-based business opportunities. So, in September 1992 the Indian government formed Antrix (an anglicized version of the Sanskrit word *antariksh*) Corporation Limited, a company that would negotiate such business agreements for ISRO. Initially, ISRO signed agreements to share data gathered by its Earth observation (EO) or remote sensing satellites. To grow this business, it launched more such satellites. Eventually, its services expanded to include technological consultancy, leasing transmission from its communication satellites and designing, building and launching satellites.

In 2020, the government opened up the space sector to private companies. Since then, hundreds of private start-ups in India have been tinkering with space technology and attracting attention and funding. Vikram-S, India's first privately built rocket developed by Skyroot Aerospace, a private aerospace manufacturer in India, lifted off from ISRO's launchpad at Sriharikota on 18 November 2022.

For a space programme that began in the 1960s, ISRO had achieved remarkable success by the turn of the century. However, one major technological obstacle in its way was developing cryogenic engines that would allow its rockets to carry heavier satellites to higher orbits.

## Troublesome Technology

Fuelled by liquid oxygen and liquid hydrogen, cryogenic engines are considered the most powerful rocket engines. ISRO wanted these engines for the Geosynchronous Satellite Launch Vehicle (GSLV)—its next launch vehicle after the

PSLV. However, acquiring cryogenic technology proved to be a formidable challenge.

Liquid oxygen and liquid hydrogen have extremely low temperatures: -183 degree Celsius and -253 degree Celsius. So, engines fuelled by them require very low-temperature engineering. Developing this technology from scratch would take decades and cost a lot of money. That's why ISRO decided to take foreign assistance, as it had for the liquid-fuel engine powering the PSLV.

Cryogenic technology was extremely expensive and the best deal that ISRO could get was from the Soviet Union. Under this deal, it procured engines that the Soviet Union had developed for a moon mission in the 1960s. The mission, however, had been called off and the engines had been lying untested, so the Soviets were willing to offer them at a considerably lower price.

The deal with the Soviets was closed in January 1991, but shortly afterwards, the contract ran into trouble. The Soviet Union—which was a group of countries led by Russia—broke up in December because of intense political unrest. The following year, the US imposed sanctions, which stopped Russia from transferring the cryogenic technology to India. A large part of the problem was the fact that the same rockets that are launched into space can also be turned into missiles and used against enemies. The US believed that India was intending to do precisely this with the cryogenic rocket it wanted to build.

These mishaps and misunderstandings ended up delaying India's quest for cryogenic technology. In 2001, India successfully tested its first GSLV, powered by a Russian engine. It was only in 2010 that ISRO was able to develop its own cryogenic engine, but the technology was based on the

Soviet engines from the 1960s and was extremely outdated. Boosting the GSLV has been an ongoing endeavour at ISRO. As of 2024, India's most advanced launch vehicle is the GSLV Mark III (also known as LVM3), which can carry a satellite of up to 4,000 kilograms into the highest orbit and up to 8,000 kilograms into LEO.

## An Indian in Space

On 12 April 1961, the Soviet test pilot Yuri Gagarin became the first human to travel into space. While Sarabhai may have marvelled at Gagarin's trip, he harboured no such ambitions for India. The technology for human spaceflight (HSF) was much too advanced, risky and prohibitively expensive for a developing nation, and did not feature in ISRO's plans at the time. So, in 1980, when India received an offer from the Soviet Union to send an Indian astronaut on an eight-day trip to space, Prime Minister Indira Gandhi approached the Indian Air Force (IAF) to find astronauts.

Around 200 IAF pilots volunteered for the programme. Shortlisted candidates were only informed of the true nature of the mission when they had to undergo intensive medical tests. Eventually, Wing Commander Rakesh Sharma became the first Indian to travel to space onboard the Soviet spacecraft *Soyuz T-11*. With him were the Soviet astronauts Yuri Malyshev and Gennady Strekalov. As the only member of the crew with no previous experience of spaceflight, Sharma's main role was to monitor instruments and conduct experiments. One of his experiments involved performing yoga in space! A highlight of his trip was the brief conversation he had with Prime Minister Indira Gandhi from space. When she asked him how India looked from space, he famously remarked, '*Saare jahan se accha*' (meaning, 'best in the world'), quoting the lyrics of a famous patriotic song in Hindi. This exchange was broadcasted on national television and led to a media frenzy. India was enthralled, but in the absence of a formal plan for HSF, Sharma's trip remained an exception.

Shortly after his return, two Indian candidates travelled to the US to undergo further tests for another HSF mission planned by NASA. But NASA called off the mission after the horrific explosion of its space shuttle *Challenger* on 28 January 1986, which claimed the lives of seven astronauts.

Indira Gandhi speaking to Rakesh Sharma

Despite this history, the allure of HSF proved hard to resist. In 2007, ISRO began the Space Capsule Recovery Experiment to test various technologies such as thermal protection, guidance, navigation and control, flotation devices and recovery needed for human space travel.

A decade later, in 2018, ISRO announced Gaganyaan—a mission to send three Indian astronauts into an orbit of 400 kilometres for three days and bring them back safely to Earth. Gaganyaan has been a giant technological leap for ISRO, particularly in terms of ensuring the safety of the crew. In October 2023, the organization carried out the first in a series of test flights planned for Gaganyaan, and in February 2024, it announced that IAF pilots Prasanth Balakrishnan Nair, Angad Pratap, Ajit Krishnan and Shubhanshu Shukla had been shortlisted for the mission.

*On 3 April 1984, Rakesh Sharma found himself seated inside the* Soyuz T-11, *facing the sky from the height of a thirteen-storey building. Describing the experience in an interview with* Brainwave *magazine, he said he could see nothing except his electronic monitor. Shortly afterwards, there were various noises and a deep rumbling below, with which the spacecraft launched into the atmosphere. The force was such that Sharma was pressed hard against his seat. Minutes later, the protective metal shroud around the rocket fell away—he was finally in space. It was still dark, but the stars were no longer twinkling points of light. The trip of a lifetime had just started!*

*Over the next eight days Sharma carried out various experiments, which included performing three or four yoga exercises such as Ustrasana (camel pose), Sithilikarana Vyayama (a set of loosening exercises) and Pranayama (breathing exercises) every day.*

*The re-entry to Earth was fiery! The spacecraft turned into a fireball, and Earth's gravity pulled hard at it. The* Soyuz T-11 *would have crashed if not for the parachute that opened up around 30,000 feet above Earth, slowing its descent. Eventually, Sharma and the two astronauts with him landed at Arkalyk in Kazakhstan.*

## Service to Humankind

Even though ISRO's missions have been a source of immense national prestige, right from its inception India's space programme has primarily aspired to benefit the ordinary people of the country. One of its earliest endeavours was the Satellite Instructional Television Experiment (SITE) in the 1970s, which used satellite transmission to broadcast educational programmes across thousands of villages in India (*also see pages 179–181*).

Shortly after SITE, which was focused on broadcasting television programmes over long distances, ISRO initiated the Satellite Telecommunications Experiments Project (STEP) to expand the use of communication satellites that could swiftly transmit information over long distances. Initially, STEP used a Franco-German satellite called Symphonie. In 1981, the first indigenous experimental communication satellite, Ariane Passenger PayLoad Experiment (APPLE), was launched by the European Space Agency. Two years later, ISRO established the Indian National Satellite (INSAT) system, one of the largest domestic communication satellite systems in the Asia-Pacific, with the successful launch of the INSAT-1B by NASA.

INSAT allowed India to broadcast radio and television programmes in far-flung places, taking the delights of early soap operas such as *Hum Log* and *Buniyaad* to scores of Indians for the very first time. Long-distance phone calls also became easier and clearer.

Apart from communications, the INSAT system also provided more accurate data on weather systems, including cloud cover, wind patterns, temperature and humidity. This helped to improve weather forecasting, monitoring cyclones, thunderstorms and monsoons and issuing timely alerts. In 2013, for example, timely and accurate warnings about Cyclone Phailin brewing over the Bay of Bengal helped save lakhs of people living along the coastal areas in Odisha and Andhra Pradesh.

Equipped to pick up and transmit distress signals from ships, aircraft and other vulnerable locations to ground stations, INSAT has also helped with rapid search and rescue operations.

In a geographically diverse country like India, information from Earth-observation or remote-sensing satellites has played a critical role in mapping, monitoring and managing natural resources. IRS-1A, India's first remote-sensing satellite, was launched in 1988 by the Soviet Union, and several others have followed. These satellites have been especially useful for farmers and fishermen who depend directly on natural resources for their livelihood. In water-scarce areas, for example, information from these satellites has helped to locate groundwater sites with greater accuracy and find appropriate locations to harvest rainwater. Similarly, fishermen have used this information to determine when and where to go fishing to get the best catch.

The Global Positioning System (GPS), a network of satellites transmitting navigation data to devices on Earth, was conceived in the US during the 1960s and covers most of the planet today. Although behind by several decades, India launched the Indian Regional Navigation Satellite System (now known as Navigation with Indian Constellation or NavIC) in 2013. It covers India and the surrounding region, extending up to 1,500 kilometres, providing accurate directions to drivers under all kinds of weather conditions and tracking the location of people and vehicles in distress.

## An Ever-Growing Endeavour

From its humble beginnings in Thumba, India's space programme has grown in leaps and bounds, bringing great pride to the nation. Its achievements have made headlines and inspired students in schools and colleges across the country to engage with space science. Since 2009, ISRO has been involved in designing, building and launching various student satellites. What might once have seemed like an outrageous adventure has today grown into a rousing demonstration of India's muscle in one of the most advanced fields of technology.

# 4

# Out in the Fields

Villages in newly independent India had an air of timelessness about them. Most people worked in farms and reared farm animals—cows, buffaloes, goats and chickens. They toiled as their forefathers had, using a variety of hand tools such as spades, pickaxes and sickles and tilled the land with a plough drawn by a pair of bullocks. They sowed seeds saved from a previous harvest and fertilized the soil with animal manure. They used water buckets and waterwheels for irrigation. The whims of the weather, however, could undo all this effort—too little rain and the harvest would dry up, too much and the fields would be flooded.

Agricultural productivity was low, but the population was rising. At the dawn of Independence, India had about 30 crore people but not enough food to feed them all. Could modern technology help with this problem? The government believed it could.

In an effort to introduce new technologies to rural India, the government initiated community development programmes in the 1950s. These programmes sought to familiarize village communities with new ways of farming and animal husbandry, aided by the expansion of electricity, water, roads and transport.

Bullocks pulling a plough

## Dammed

Back in 1947, less than 20 per cent of India's farms were irrigated. So, the government decided to build large, multipurpose dams that would not only bring more water to India's farms but also produce hydroelectricity for its industries. Such dams were very popular in the US and the Soviet Union, and now, even India could boast of them. The most prestigious of these was the Bhakra Dam on the river Sutlej, set to become the world's second-highest dam of the time upon completion. It would generate about 10 lakh kilowatts of electricity and irrigate over 70 lakh acres of land through a vast network of canals connected to its reservoir. In 1963, when the dam was finally functional, Prime Minister Jawaharlal Nehru proudly dedicated it to the nation, calling it 'the new temple . . . of India'.

However, it was the battle against crippling shortages of food grains and milk that truly brought a technological revolution in India's farms.

## Farm Revolutions

**About 51%**

of India's farms were covered by irrigation in 2024

During the 1960s, India's food crisis turned into a nightmare. Following disagreements with the Indian government, the USA ended its supply of cheap food grains to India. Meanwhile, back-to-back droughts destroyed the local harvest. Food prices soared, and riots broke out in many places as hungry people looted grains in desperation—something had to be done urgently.

Chidambaram Subramaniam (L) and M.S. Swaminathan (R)

Chidambaram Subramaniam, the new minister of food and agriculture, and M.S. Swaminathan, an agricultural scientist assisting him, had heard of something extraordinary that had happened in Mexico during the 1950s. Agricultural scientists led by Norman Borlaug had developed a variety of wheat that produced two to three times more grain than ordinary wheat, ushering in the Green Revolution. By 1964, a country that once imported half of its wheat was producing enough to export five lakh tonnes! Subramaniam and Swaminathan decided to bring these high-yielding seeds to India.

Not everyone was convinced about this plan. Many wondered if Indian agriculture could weather this technological change. But the food crisis was so acute that there appeared to be no other option.

The seeds arrived in India in 1965. Swaminathan began directing Indian scientists on how to adapt the Mexican wheat variety to Indian conditions and make it 'chapati-ready'! Demonstrations and trials were held in fields, and promotions were done on All India Radio.

Powered by chemical fertilizers and pesticides, modern irrigation systems and farm machinery, the high-yielding seeds of the Green Revolution brought a scientifically and technologically advanced way of farming to India. Not only was it entirely different from traditional farming, but it was also more costly. So, the seeds were initially introduced in places like Punjab, which had a relatively prosperous class of farmers who owned large tracts of well-irrigated land and had access to electricity. The government also offered a variety of benefits (subsidies and incentives) to encourage the adoption of the new seeds. It reduced the prices of seeds, fertilizers and pesticides, slashed the cost of electricity to pump out groundwater for irrigation, and fixed a Minimum Support Price at which it would buy the produce to make it available for public distribution.

Enticed by this agricultural package and the promise of high yields, farmers began to enthusiastically take up the ways of the Green Revolution. By the 1970s, India was producing enough food grains to feed its population, and, eventually, it became a leading exporter of these grains.

## Technologies of the Green Revolution

### Scientifically Developed Seeds

Every plant starts from a seed, and each seed comes with tiny instructions—genes—that decide how the plant will grow. Genes tell a plant what colour its leaves will be, how tall it will grow and whether it will survive in dry or wet weather conditions. In nature, genes can change on their own over time. For example, the genes of a wild plant might naturally change to make it more resistant to drought or pests. Farmers have cleverly used these natural changes to their advantage for centuries, by selecting the best seeds to plant in the next season. This method of selection is called selective breeding. Scientists of the Green Revolution used selective breeding techniques to develop high-yielding varieties of wheat and rice. However, unlike traditional seeds, farmers could not save these scientifically developed seeds from one harvest to sow them in the next—the yields would not be the same. So, they had to buy new seeds each season.

Since the Green Revolution, scientists in India have developed several different varieties of seeds to improve yields, resist pests and withstand harsh climatic conditions.

## Seed Engineering

With advances in biotechnology (combining biology and technology to solve problems, create new products and improve human lives), scientists found a way of introducing genes from an entirely different organism into a seed. This is called Genetic Modification.

In 2002, for the first time, the government allowed the cultivation of a genetically modified crop in India—Bt Cotton. The seeds of Bt Cotton contain genes from a soil-dwelling bacterium, *Bacillus thuringiensis* (Bt), which makes the crop toxic to some common pests like the cotton bollworm. This led to a significant increase in cotton yields and spurred a biotechnology revolution in India. Many people, however, are concerned about such modification, especially in the seeds of food crops. They worry about the impact this might have on the environment, the human body and the cost of farming. More recently, scientists have started using gene-editing—making small changes in genes without adding anything from another species.

### Chemical Fertilizers and Pesticides

Animal manure and organic pesticides, such as those made from neem and walnut leaves, would not work on the Green Revolution seeds. Farmers needed to use chemical fertilizers to fertilize the soil and chemical pesticides to ward off pests.

Farmer spraying chemical pesticide in a field

Electric tube well

### Irrigation

Relying on the rains was no longer feasible. Fields needed to be watered at the right time with the right amount of water. Many farmers installed electric tube wells in their farms to pump out groundwater.

### Farm Machines

As agricultural produce increased, more and more farmers were willing to use modern machines for farm work. Demand for tractors that could pull and push mechanical devices for different types of farm work, such as ploughing and harvesting, began to rise. Sensing an opportunity, the Central Mechanical Engineering Research Institute, a national laboratory under the Council of Scientific & Industrial Research (CSIR), developed Swaraj, India's first indigenous tractor. It used less power than foreign tractors and could operate more effectively in the small farms owned by the majority of Indian farmers.

Launched in 1974, Swaraj became an instant success due to its low cost and ease of maintenance. Its success encouraged other Indian companies to manufacture tractors and by the 1980s, India was not just making and selling tractors locally but was also exporting them to other countries.

Swaraj tractor

Even as the Green Revolution swept across fields in northern India, the beginnings of a milk revolution were brewing in Anand, a sleepy little town in Gujarat. An enterprising cooperative of dairy farmers led by Tribhuvandas Patel in the Kaira District of Anand had joined forces with Verghese Kurien, a dairy professional, and Harichand Dalaya, a dairy technologist, to set up a thriving milk business.

By 1952, the Kaira District Co-operative Milk Producer's Union Limited, now known as AMUL (Anand Milk Union Limited), was producing nearly 20,000 litres of milk. Supply had outstripped demand, and the farmers needed a processing plant that could turn the surplus milk into milk powder, which was easy to preserve and could be turned back into milk during the summer, when buffaloes produced lower quantities. But there was one hurdle. Unlike other dairy-producing countries, like Australia and New Zealand, which got their milk from cows, India primarily got its milk from buffaloes. So far, no one had attempted to make milk powder from buffalo milk. In 1954, Dalaya made a technological breakthrough by inventing the first drier to turn liquid buffalo milk into powder. This paved the way for the first dairy plant in the world to mass-manufacture milk powder from buffalo milk. It was also the first time in the history of independent India that farmers owned the most technologically advanced dairy in the country.

How was AMUL thriving when nearly all other dairies in India had failed and the country was facing a milk crisis? During the 1960s, Prime Minister Lal Bahadur Shastri turned to Verghese Kurien for an answer, and the answer was quite simple. Unlike the other dairies, which were either owned by the government or by private vendors, AMUL was owned by dairy farmers. The farmers chose their leaders, who hired professionals like Kurien to run the business. When AMUL did well, the farmers benefitted the most. The prime minister was extremely excited. If AMUL's success was not because of any special conditions prevailing in Anand, its model could be replicated elsewhere too.

In 1970, the Anand Model of cooperative dairying was scaled up to help India overcome its milk shortage. Large dairies were set up in major cities such as Bombay (now Mumbai), Delhi, Calcutta (now Kolkata) and Madras (now Chennai). These dairies got their milk from cooperative dairying areas, known as milksheds, that followed the Anand Model. Known as Operation Flood or the White Revolution, this was the biggest dairy-development project in the world. It empowered dairy farmers, promoted technologically advanced dairying and turned India into the largest milk-producing nation in the world in 1998.

### Rainbow Revolution

The success of the Green and White Revolutions encouraged similar revolutions that applied modern science and technology to expand the production of various kinds of food, including oilseeds, fish, fruits, eggs, potatoes and meat. These came to be collectively called the Rainbow Revolution.

## From Farm to Table

The food that we eat doesn't typically reach us as soon as it's harvested. It usually makes a long journey before it arrives on our table. This journey includes a number of different steps, such as sorting, storing, transporting, processing and packaging. However, there is a big challenge along the way—food is highly perishable and can spoil quickly.

To effectively fight food shortages, India also needed to find ways to stop such wastage. For this, it needed to promote post-harvest technologies that prevented harvested food from spoiling and increased its life. Some early examples of such technologies were traditional *atta chakkis* that ground harvested wheat into flour, *ghanis* that extracted oil from oil seeds and insulated railway vans used for transporting milk.

Things began to change in the 1960s and 1970s, when the Green and White Revolutions led to a huge increase in food production. Suddenly, there was a lot more food, but not enough ways to store and transport it safely. In 1968, for example, the Green Revolution produced such a bumper harvest that the government struggled to store and distribute the surplus food grains. Workers in storehouses went on strike because they were overworked and thousands of bags of food grains were ruined by rain and rats before they could reach anyone!

The need for post-harvest technologies had become urgent and the government pushed for them. Since then, India has made significant strides in developing such technologies.

In a country where the climate tends to be hot and humid most of the time, improvements in the 'cold chain' (refrigerated storage, transportation and display) have made it possible to preserve a variety of perishable food and transport it over longer distances. Developments in packaging have meant that most of our food comes packed in plastic today, which shields it from moisture and micro-organisms. One of the most visible advances in post-harvest technologies is seen in the endless variety of food products in grocery stores. From food mixes to instant noodles, these products are usually highly processed and packed with additives to make them last longer and taste just right!

Feeding a populous country like India has meant that not only farming, but even the journey that food makes from farms to our tables has become a lot more high-tech than it used to be.

# From Potatoes to Potato Chips

Potatoes are harvested by farmers

Harvested potatoes are kept in sacks and usually stored in cold storage

Sacks of potatoes are transported to a factory for processing

Potatoes reach the factory where they are turned into potato chips

Ready packets of potato chips are sent to the market

## Environmental Fallouts

Nearly all new technologies introduced in Indian agriculture since Independence have had ecological fallouts. Some of the earliest and most prominent environmental protests in India were against large dams that obstructed free-flowing rivers, drowned land and displaced people. These protests made governments more conscious of the social and environmental impacts of damming.

Overuse of pesticides and water in the wake of the Green Revolution led to wastage of resources, chemical contamination and a massive depletion in the quality of the soil over time. The White Revolution increased the number of dairy animals in India, leading to problems like overgrazing, while the expansion of post-harvest technologies amplified electricity consumption and created mountains of waste made up of plastic packaging.

Such issues prompted a variety of actions by farmers, social organizations and the government. Among the earliest responses to the problems of the Green Revolution came in the 1980s from farmers in Jardhargaon, a small village in Uttarakhand (then part of Uttar Pradesh). Troubled by failing soils and the high cost of buying seeds, chemical fertilizers and pesticides, the farmers of the village began the *Beej Bachao Andolan* or Save the Seeds movement, to go back to growing local varieties of rice, kidney beans and other kinds of crops, without using any chemicals. Over time, such ideas spread around the country.

Seed banks to save indigenous varieties of crops took root in different states, and in 1996, a National Gene Bank was established at the National Bureau of Plant Genetic Resources in Delhi. During the early 2000s, the state of Sikkim began an ambitious programme to give up chemical agriculture and shift to organic farming. The local government began training programmes for farmers and helped them to switch to bio-fertilizers, compost and traditional ways of managing pests. It also helped the farmers to market their produce. By 2016, Sikkim had become India's first fully organic state. Other states, too, have been actively encouraging the reduction of chemicals in farming.

Meanwhile, in 2015, the government began supplying urea coated with neem oil to all farmers. Urea is the main fertilizer used in India, and the neem oil coating has helped to control soil contamination caused by the chemicals in it.

Before the Green Revolution, millets were commonly grown in India. Not only were they more nutritious than the other high-yielding grains but they also used less water, fertilizer and pesticide, grew well in dry conditions and could withstand extreme weather. However, following the Green Revolution, millet cultivation began to fall. In light of the challenges facing Indian agriculture, the government decided to reintroduce these coarse cereals to Indian farms and food in 2013. Later on, 2018 was declared the 'National Year of Millets' and the government began offering a Minimum Support Price to encourage more farmers to cultivate them. From midday meals in government schools to food in Indian railways, millets were actively promoted for consumption.

To fight the shortage of good quality fodder caused by overgrazing, farmers in many parts of India started cultivating plants like Azolla, an aquatic, floating fern that grows quickly, easily and cheaply, to feed their animals. Meanwhile, in a bid to cut down plastic usage, milk producers like Mother Dairy began encouraging consumers to switch to token or 'loose milk' from their vending machines, which is cheaper than packet milk.

## Technology to the Rescue?

Even though it has caused many problems, technology has also offered ways of overcoming them. Precision farming that uses precise amounts of water and chemicals, for instance, was one way of conserving resources. Among the earliest technologies used for precision farming was drip irrigation.

In the past, bamboo pipes were used in parts of North-east India to drip precise amounts of water on plants. Modern drip irrigation came to India in the 1970s from Israel, where engineer and inventor Simcha Blass had developed a network of plastic pipes from which water, as well as liquid fertilizers and pesticides, would drip slowly and directly on the roots of plants. Initially, the technology appeared strange and complicated to many Indian farmers. It was also extremely costly to install and maintain, especially in small farms. But in an effort to control rising water wastage and fight droughts, many state governments began promoting it. In the late 1980s, water-stressed Maharashtra became the first state to support drip irrigation, and by 2017, it had made this mandatory for growing sugarcane, a water-guzzling crop. Over the years, many other states have also turned to this technology. Today, lakhs of hectares of land in India are covered by drip irrigation, and even though this is still a fraction of the total land under irrigation, it has proved especially useful for farmers growing delicate crops like fruits, vegetables and flowers.

Apart from precision farming, in recent years, the government has also been actively encouraging the use of solar-powered devices in rural India to meet electricity needs

Drip irrigation in a field

in eco-friendly and cost-effective ways (*also see pages 214–218*). This has been beneficial for farmers across various states. Solar refrigerators, for instance, have helped dairy cooperatives in the desert state of Rajasthan to preserve surplus milk and earn more from their produce. Advances in satellite-based remote sensing during the 1980s and the Global Positioning Satellite (GPS) service in the 1990s helped India survey its vast farmland, track the weather and collect information that was hugely beneficial for farming (*also see page 68*). Yet, it was the development of telecommunications (*also see page 130*) that played a significant role in disseminating this information, as well as news on useful technologies and government initiatives in rural India.

In the early 2000s, resource centres were opened in villages across the country where the Internet and telephone were used to pass on agricultural information to farmers. Soon afterwards, mobile-based services brought such information directly into the hands of farmers. In 2009, the Indian Council for Research on International Economic Relations conducted a study to assess the impact of mobile phones on agricultural productivity. Nearly all the farmers who took part in it reported that getting information through mobile phones was convenient and had helped them reduce costs.

## Odds and Opportunities

In the years since Independence, a number of technologies have been introduced in Indian agriculture. However, the adoption of these technologies in farming remains uneven.

A majority of India's farmers own small lands (less than two hectares), few farm animals and have limited earnings. According to a 2021–2022 survey by the National Bank for Agriculture and Rural Development, households in rural India, on an average, earn less than 13,000 rupees per month. So, an obvious hurdle facing the adoption of new technologies is cost. Often, such technologies are just too expensive for ordinary farmers to afford. Although the government and various social organizations offer subsidies to reduce the cost of different kinds of technologies, this is not always enough to motivate farmers. They also need to feel convinced about the advantages of new technologies before adopting them. So, how does one convince them? By creating technologies that bear their interests in mind and effectively communicating the advantages of using these technologies to them. Unfortunately, this is easier said than done.

In 2015, for example, the government invested crores of rupees in a soil health card scheme. Under this scheme, farmers got access to cards which provided them information on the health of their soil and recommended suitable crops and fertilizers. However, as experts pointed out, these recommendations weren't always useful for farmers. Some of the recommended fertilizers, for instance, were expensive and would increase the cost of farming. Moreover, the recommendations tended to be conveyed in a highly technical way, unsuitable for ordinary farmers.

Food is a fuel for life, and farmers are its primary producers. So, any technology that seeks to revolutionize food, needs to also empower farmers. In the world's most populous country, where a majority of people work in agriculture, this presents an incredible opportunity for technology to bring truly extraordinary change, not just by helping to produce more food while conserving resources but by uplifting crores of ordinary farmers in this pursuit.

*Rahul Sharma is an unusual farmer. He holds a degree in computer science and has worked with technology companies for more than two decades. But in 2016, when the techie finally returned to Punjab to take up farming on his ancestral land, he found himself struggling with technology on the field.*

*Technology had come to Punjab's fields in a big way after the Green Revolution. However, it soon became clear to Rahul that the machines and the rest of the farming ecosystem were only suitable for the Green Revolution varieties of wheat and rice and not for the crops he was growing.*

*'I grow* khapli *(Emmer) wheat, an ancient variety that has a thick layer of husk. The combine harvester that separates the grain from the husk is not suitable for this variety. Because of this, I have to put the harvested grains through another round of dehusking, which is not easy because people handling the machine say that it will get damaged as it is not designed to dehusk* khapli*. I also grow* desi mung *dal which cannot be harvested in one go because the mung beans do not ripen at the same time. The ones on top of the stalk are ripe and ready to be picked. But the ones below are green, and you have to wait for them to ripen. If you wait for all the beans to ripen, a lot gets wasted. But the machines made for harvesting are not able to harvest just the ripe portion. Sowing and harvesting are backbreaking activities—I've tried doing them with my cousins and none of us could cope.'*

*Since he began farming, Rahul has faced many setbacks. Many times, entire harvests have gone to waste because there were no suitable machines! What of farm hands?*

*'Farm labour—mostly migrant workers—is in short supply because most of them are engaged in other jobs in cities. Those who do come to work in agriculture prefer to work at the state* mandis*, as it gives them an assured income for a longer duration. Getting people to work on farms is very hard and costs much more than using machines.'*

*'We need machines in farming,' he says. However, he is quick to add that they need to be designed to suit the needs of all farmers, and not just those following the ways of the Green Revolution. In a country like India, which has different kinds of soils and climates, farmers grow many different crops and people manufacturing farm equipment need to speak to different groups of farmers, observe their work and create machines that serve their needs. Foisting machines on farmers will not help.*

*Rahul is convinced that promoting crop diversity is the need of the hour. But instead of encouraging farmers to grow other, more suitable types of crops, the government continues to push paddy (rice). 'Water levels in Punjab have fallen so low—it should not be growing a water-guzzling crop like paddy at all. But instead of reducing the area sown under paddy, the government is introducing machines and policies to manage crop residue. Not all farmers can afford these machines, which leaves them with no option than to burn the paddy straw, leading to air pollution.*

*'Moreover, the mills that polish rice remove all its nutritious bran and then the food companies fortify the rice with artificial nutrients—first you take away the nutrients from the natural food and then you try to fortify it artificially!'*

*Although such problems frustrate him from time to time, Rahul carries on. Farming, after all, is his heritage and land is his gold.*

# 5

# Electronic Revolution

By the 1960s, India had built giant factories and large dams. It had embarked on technologically advanced nuclear and space programmes. Technology had also entered its farms in the form of the scientifically developed seeds of the Green Revolution. But one critical area remained in need of urgent attention—electronics.

Even though Bharat Electronics Limited (BEL) had been set up in 1954, the production of electronics remained inadequate, and this inadequacy became embarrassingly obvious during the 1962 war with China (*also see page 28*). India found itself severely lacking electronic instruments, such as advanced radar and communication systems, that modern warfare relied on. So, in the midst of war, India turned its attention to electronics and scrambled to address this pressing technological gap.

The Atomic Research Centre, later renamed the Bhabha Atomic Research Centre (BARC), which was working on India's nuclear programme, had made a modest beginning in acquiring electronics that it needed for its work. So, the government called upon Homi Bhabha, who was heading India's nuclear programme, to lead a committee that would assess the 'total electronics requirements of the country'. The committee was set up in 1963, and over the next three years, it compiled the first comprehensive report on the state of electronics in India. By 1966 the government had a definite sense of the poor state of India's electronics industry and what it needed to do to fix it.

The very next year, the government set up another company—Electronics Corporation of India Limited (ECIL)—to develop a wide range of electronics, from small components to large devices. By 1970, India also had an Electronics Commission and a Department of Electronics that reported directly to the prime minister. Yet there was a persistent problem plaguing the development of electronics—and it wasn't technological.

## Powering Electronics

An electric current is extremely powerful and can cause a life-threatening shock. So, the flow of electricity must be carefully controlled when used to run machines. Controlling the flow of electricity is the job of the electric circuit, which you will find inside all electronic devices. The moment you switch on any electronic device, the components that make up its circuit

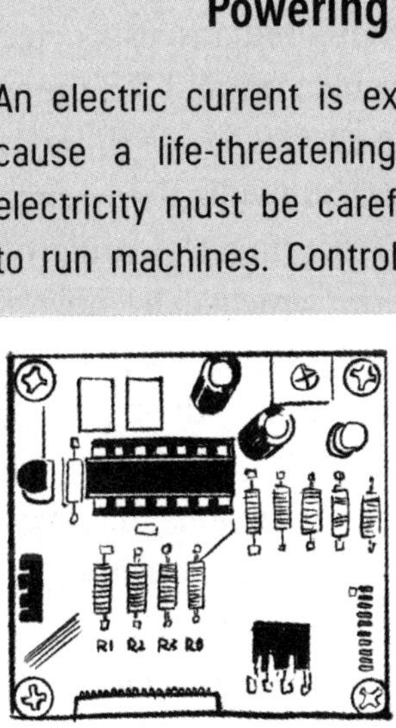

kick into action, controlling and directing the current flowing through it.

Voltage or volts is a measure of the force driving the current. Electricity in Indian households is typically 220 volts, so most appliances are made to handle this voltage. Anything more than this will damage your device.

## The Electronics Gap

India had a pressing need for electronics in defence, nuclear and space technologies, but the greatest driver of the industry was consumer electronics. If more Indians used electronic devices, it would lead to increasing demand for the various components needed to make the circuits inside these devices. However, the government was unwilling to encourage ordinary Indians from actively adopting electronic devices. In a predominantly rural country wracked by poverty and illiteracy, the government viewed such devices as luxuries and imposed heavy taxes on them, making them prohibitively expensive. Back in 1956, for example, Prime Minister Jawaharlal Nehru had said: 'I am not anxious that everybody in India should have a motor car or, say, a washing machine or a refrigerator.'

Lack of consumer demand meant that few businesses were willing to manufacture electronic components in India on a large scale. Meanwhile, taxes on imports made it challenging to acquire these parts from abroad. To make matters worse, the government also rejected several manufacturing proposals involving foreign electronic makers such as Texas Instruments and Fairchild Semiconductors. Electronic manufacturers were in a dilemma: how were they to go about their business under such circumstances?

Among those troubled by such restrictions was Vinay Bharat Ram, the scion of Delhi Cloth Mills (DCM), a large industrial group in north India. In his book, *The Long Revolution: The Birth and Growth of India's IT Industry*, journalist Dinesh C. Sharma writes that Vinay had his eyes set on electronics, specifically an electronic calculator that was being touted as the 'star of business machines' during the 1960s. So, he imported the gadget developed by Sharp Electronics in Japan and got a team of engineers to disassemble it to see if they could reassemble it locally. Keen to collaborate with a Japanese company, Vinay flew to Japan and managed to secure a meeting with Akio Morita at Sony (who would eventually become famous as the man behind the iconic Sony Walkman).

Vinay's company had no experience in the technology business, but his father, Lala Bharat Ram had just become the first Asian President of the International Chamber of Commerce. This impressed the Japanese and they agreed for Vinay's company, DCM Data Products, to assemble 2,000 Sony electronic calculators in India. This was the first industrial collaboration for making a high-tech electronic device in the country. But the government was having none of it and refused to allow a manufacturing deal involving a foreign company.

Left with no option, the team of engineers at DCM Data Products reverse-engineered the Sharp calculator as best as they could. Without foreign know-how and easy access to electronic components, the manufacturing process was outdated. Parts were hand-wired and could malfunction easily, and the calculator was housed within a bulky wooden casing, making it slightly larger than a briefcase. Nevertheless, this locally made electronic calculator was proudly shown to Prime Minister Indira Gandhi as an example of indigenous technology at the India International Trade Fair in 1972.

## Reverse Engineering

Imagine you find a cool gadget, but you don't know anything about it. How would you figure it out? One way of doing this is through reverse engineering. This means carefully disassembling the gadget to study its parts, understand how they function and see how they're connected. Engineers and scientists often use reverse engineering to learn how something was made and then produce something similar or better. The practice has been especially common in developing countries like India, which industrialized later than developed nations. Without easy access to advanced technology or manufacturing knowledge, these countries often had to reverse-engineer imported products to build their versions, reduce dependence on foreign technology, and develop local industries.

In 1973, the government established India's first Special Economic Zone (SEZ) for electronics in Santacruz, Mumbai.

It hoped to bring together Indian electronic manufacturers under one roof and offer them special incentives to manufacture and export electronics. But this didn't address the key issues faced by the industry.

The government's refusal to acknowledge the need for consumer electronics had not only created problems for the electronics industry but was also against the tide of the times. Despite all the government's restrictions, by the 1970s, the march of modern technology was beginning to reach the doorstep of ordinary Indian households, and an electronics revolution was in the making—powered by a growing appetite for consumer electronics. Leading the way was the humble radio that brought everything from news, sports, education and entertainment to ordinary Indians.

## Radio Revolution

The radio had been introduced in India during the 1920s. Based entirely on foreign technology, the earliest radio broadcasts were made by elite radio clubs in Bombay (now Mumbai), Calcutta (now Kolkata) and Madras (now Chennai). But these broadcasts proved to be too costly and had to be discontinued. Eventually, the British Government in India took up radio broadcasting and started the Indian State Broadcasting Service in 1930, which was renamed All India Radio (AIR) in 1936.

AIR (also known as Akashvani) had nine stations, of which three went to Pakistan following the Partition in 1947. The remaining stations in Delhi, Mumbai, Kolkata, Chennai, Tiruchirappalli and Lucknow reached about 11 per cent of the population through an estimated 2.75 lakh radio sets. In a country where the majority could not read or write, radio was an important means of delivering vital information to the masses. So, the government decided to open more broadcasting stations across the country. However, what truly transformed radio and, indeed, the entire field of electronics was the transistor—a tiny electronic component that could strengthen and control the electronic signal passing through a circuit.

An old-fashioned radio set manufactured by the British company Murphy—one of the leading suppliers of radio sets in newly independent India. A Murphy radio was also featured in the title song of the 2012 Hindi movie *Barfi*!

Before the coming of transistors, bulky vacuum tubes were used to control current. These tubes consumed a lot of power and were prone to frequent overheating. In 1947, physicists John Bardeen, Walter Houser Brattain and William Bradford Shockley at Bell Laboratories in the US invented the transistor, which replaced vacuum tubes. Not only was the transistor more reliable and efficient, but it was also much smaller, leading to the creation of small and portable electronic devices, such as transistor radios and mobile phones, that could be carried around in a pocket or purse.

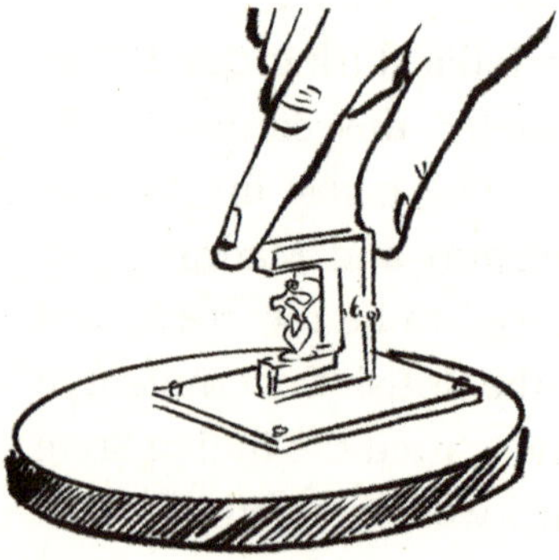

A replica of the first transistor that marked such a significant advance in the field of electronics that its inventors were awarded a Nobel Prize in 1956.

Transistor radios came to India around 1958. Within a decade, newspapers were reporting about farmers going into their fields with transistor radios slung on their shoulders. In a speech at Roorkee University, even Prime Minister Indira Gandhi admitted that a transistor radio in the hands of a bullock-cart driver was no longer an uncommon sight. She also acknowledged that apart from information and music, the radio was 'a symbol of modernity and the world of plenty'. By 1970, despite the government's disinterest in promoting consumer electronics, India had around 20 lakh radio sets for personal use.

A model of a transistor radio—the first portable electronic device available in India.

Radio broadcasts in the early decades in India used Amplitude Modulation (AM) transmission, which involved relatively inexpensive technology, consumed less power and could travel over long distances. But it was often plagued by static—hissing, clicking, grinding sounds that interrupted the broadcast. This problem was addressed in the 1970s with Frequency Modulation (FM) transmission. It had fewer interruptions, which resulted in a significantly better listening experience.

Till the 1990s, the government maintained strict control over radio broadcasts. But in 1995, the Supreme Court ruled that the airwaves were public property, and the government could not monopolize them. That's how, in 2001, India got its first private FM radio station—Radio City Bangalore. After that, there was no turning back. Radio broadcasts increased and content became more varied.

The reach of radio expanded in 2002 when the government began granting permissions for setting up low-power, hyperlocal community radio stations. One of the first community radio stations was established at Anna University in Chennai in 2004. It catered to the needs of people residing around the university with broadcasts on issues such as healthcare, hygiene, female literacy and employment. Since then, community radio stations have multiplied across towns and districts in India.

Meanwhile, with the coming of the Internet in the 1990s, radio broadcasts gradually became digital and available on demand—people could now listen to them at any time they wanted on the Internet!

Today, people no longer need a separate device to listen to radio broadcasts. They can listen to them on car stereos and even on mobile phones. The number of Indian homes with a radio set has declined dramatically, but with over 380 private FM radio channels in more than 110 cities and more than 370 community radio stations, radio coverage reaches nearly 99 per cent of the population! Its incredible reach is highlighted by the fact that despite the availability of several other kinds of media, Prime Minister Narendra Modi began a monthly radio programme, *Mann ki Baat*, in 2014 to interact with citizens on various issues concerning the nation.

## Pulse of the People

Entertainment led the way when it came to the rising popularity of consumer electronics in India. The phenomenal spread of the radio was followed closely by the television, which grabbed eyeballs and hooked Indians to visual entertainment. Different polls and surveys in the 1970s showed that access to radio and television had a profound impact on how Indians viewed technology and its role in their lives. Many Indians had an extremely positive outlook on technological progress and felt that technology would transform life in fundamental ways—curing cancer, accurately predicting the weather and permitting interplanetary travel, among other things.

By the 1980s, the government, too, had picked up on this. What followed were trailblazing policies that did away with many restrictions on consumer electronics and encouraged private companies to manufacture electronic components either on their own or in collaboration with the government. These policies increased the number of electronics companies in India and, by the 1990s, different types of electronic devices began to enter more and more Indian homes. Some of these devices, such as the computer and the mobile phone (*also see pages 134–138*), went on to unleash full-fledged technological revolutions in the country.

The electronics industry, however, had suffered because of the government's initial reluctance to promote consumer electronics. By the time the government finally lifted restrictions in the 1980s, local production had fallen so far behind that importing was cheaper than developing electronics from scratch. As a result, the Indian market was flooded with foreign components and devices.

Although the situation has improved since then, India's electronics industry continues to rely heavily on imports. In fact, according to some experts, after oil, coal and natural gas—required to meet the country's energy needs—India spends the most on importing electronics. Given the widespread and ever-growing use of electronics across various industries, unless this situation is addressed, India's electronics bill may well exceed its energy bill.

Various initiatives have been taken by governments since the 1980s to address this shortfall, but success has remained limited. 'Make in India', launched in 2014, is the most recent government initiative in this direction. It aims to transform

India into a global design and manufacturing hub across various fields, including electronics. Aided by significant improvements in electricity supply, road development and other key infrastructure, as well as India's growing economic might, 'Make in India' has a greater possibility of succeeding than past efforts.

## 'Fab-ulous' Chips

At the heart of every electronic device in the world today lies a type of transistor called a semiconductor, microchip or an integrated circuit. One of India's key ambitions under 'Make in India' is to design and manufacture semiconductors and become one of the top five semiconductor chip producers globally by 2029. This, though, is an enormous undertaking.

First, one needs to design these semiconductor chips. This requires highly skilled engineers, extensive research and development, and access to technical know-how, which is often protected by laws. Many well-known chipmakers in the world have spent decades perfecting designs that reduce the size of a semiconductor chip.

Once a design has been finalized, countries need a semiconductor fabrication unit (or fab) where these chips can be mass-produced. These facilities are highly controlled environments with extremely low levels of pollutants, ultra-pure water, chemicals and gases. They require trained workers and massive amounts of monetary investment—setting up a fab can cost billions of dollars. So, governments need to offer exceptionally attractive benefits to encourage chipmakers to set up such facilities.

In the past, India made several attempts to set up fabs. Some never took off, while others found limited success. After the 1962 war, BEL started a fab, but during the 1980s, it lost out to cheaper, high-quality imports from China, Taiwan and South Korea. In the mid-1980s, another fab was established in partnership with BEL. This partnership could have gone a long way in aiding India's electronics industry, but it didn't get enough government support and was eventually abandoned. An ambitious semiconductor complex was established in Chandigarh around the same time. It began by manufacturing 5,000 nanometre chips and quickly advanced to produce 800 nanometre chips. This was close to the cutting edge of the technology at that time. However, the entire complex was gutted in a mysterious fire in 1989, setting back India's progress by more than a decade. India's space programme revived the complex to manufacture a limited number of chips for its work. But this was barely a shadow of the original complex. In mid-2005, a major multinational company tried starting operations in south India, but insufficient government interest prompted it to take the project to China, which lapped up the opportunity. This episode also discouraged other multinational corporations looking at investing in fabs in India.

Semiconductor technology changes rapidly, and the delays and setbacks have cost India dearly. In 2021, the government made another effort towards semiconductor manufacturing by launching the India Semiconductor Mission as part of its 'Make in India' initiative. Under this mission, it laid the foundation of three semiconductor factories in 2024—a fab in Dholera, Gujarat, and two assembly, testing, marking and packaging facilities in Sanand, Gujarat, and Morigaon, Assam.

The first chip from the fab in Dholera is expected to roll out in 2026. While it won't be super advanced, it will mark a major milestone in India's electronics history.

# 6

# Computing Comes of Age

Newly independent India's greatest ambition was to improve the lives of its people. But to do this, the government needed to know them better. How exactly did ordinary Indians live? What kind of work did they do? How much did they earn from their work? How did they spend their money? There were many questions and hardly any answers. Without this information, it would be difficult for the government to decide how best to allocate its expenses to help the people. So, in 1950, the government began one of the greatest information-gathering exercises the world had ever seen—the National Sample Survey.

Back in 1950, India had more than five lakh villages and over 30 crore people. Collecting information about all of them would have been impossible. So, the survey team carefully chose 1,833 villages across the country, and between October 1950 and March 1951, over 600 surveyors travelled through India, interviewing people, observing farmlands and measuring yields. By the end of the exercise, they had gathered enormous amounts of information about the lives of ordinary Indians. But how were they going to chart and analyse all of this data in time to present the government with a picture of the lives of ordinary people in the country?

Prasanta Chandra Mahalanobis, a serious-looking scientist who was leading the survey, decided to use an 'electronic brain'. That's how independent India set out on a quest to get its first computer.

### The Human Computer Style

SHAKUNTALA DEVI

Before computers were deployed, humans were hired to perform numerous complex calculations. This wasn't an easy task and needed an exceptional flair for mathematics. Indian mathematician Shakuntala Devi was called a Human Computer because of her extraordinary ability to make lengthy mathematical calculations in her head. On 18 June 1980, she entered the Guinness Book of World Records for the fastest human computation by correctly multiplying two thirteen-digit numbers in twenty-eight seconds!

## Chasing Computers

During the 1950s, the computer was a new and rare kind of technology—a calculating machine that could process a large amount of data in a short period to produce understandable results. It promised fabulous possibilities and inspired much awe. Most countries coveted it, but it was so notoriously expensive that few could afford it. Mahalanobis, however, needed a computer urgently—India had decided to conduct National Sample Surveys periodically, and only a computer could get through all that data in time.

In 1950, an Electronic Computer Laboratory was set up at the Indian Statistical Institute (ISI) in Calcutta (now Kolkata), founded by Mahalanobis. He hired two young graduates, Samarendra Kumar Mitra and Soumyendra Mohan Bose, to assemble a computer from scratch. This was an extremely difficult task because the parts were not readily available in India and importing them would have been too costly. Left with no other choice, Mitra and Bose scoured through scrap markets and disposal depots, salvaging useful materials from leftover machines of World War II and cobbled together India's first analogue computer by 1953.

Although Mahalanobis was proud of the fact that the ISI had managed to build a computer despite formidable odds, he was acutely aware of the machine's technical limitations. So, even as he nurtured the design and engineering teams at the ISI, Mahalanobis continued to hunt for more advanced computers anxiously. That's how he came upon the Hollerith Electronic Computer (HEC), which was being marketed by the British Tabulating Machine (BTM) Company, and decided to place an order.

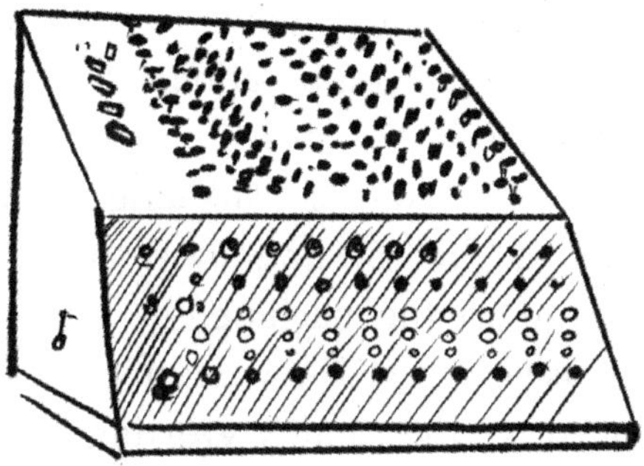

The analogue computer assembled by Mitra and Bose at ISI had rotating keys, which had to be manually set up at particular values to calculate results that were punched on cards.

For a princely sum of around 2,00,000 rupees, BTM agreed to custom-build India's first digital computer, the HEC-2M, in 1954. Since this was the only such machine that India was purchasing, it wasn't feasible for BTM to maintain it. So, the ISI sent two of its engineers, Mohi Mukherjee and Amaresh Roy, to Letchworth in England to observe how the computer was being built and learn how to operate and maintain it. In 1956, the HEC-2M finally arrived in India. Mukherjee and Roy spent two months assembling it, based on notes from their training in England and sometimes on instinct. The computer was so big that it took up an entire floor at the ISI! Since it wasn't designed to cope with the humidity of Kolkata, the computer was placed in an air-conditioned area, which, too, was a novelty at the time.

By today's standards, the HEC-2M had incredibly low computing power. It could only perform up to 200 additions or five multiplications per second (modern computers can perform lakhs of calculations in a millisecond!) and wasn't easy to use. Nevertheless, it performed complex calculations on the National Sample Survey data, served other divisions at the ISI and even fulfilled computational requests from other scientific institutes in India. Most importantly, it initiated a budding computing culture as Mukherjee and Roy trained other engineers at the ISI and even created instruction manuals on how to use the machine.

Despite its uses, the HEC-2M wasn't advanced enough to meet the needs of the rapidly growing National Sample Survey data, and Mahalanobis soon ordered another big computer—the Ural-1 (named after a mountain range in present-day Russia)—from the Soviet Union, using financial assistance from the United Nations. Ural-1 arrived in India in 1958, followed closely by eight Soviet engineers who took three months to assemble it. The engineers also held training sessions for Indian engineers in the construction, operation and maintenance of the computer. By 1959, Ural-1 was hard at work, its printer reportedly making 'ridiculous noises'. Even as the ISI cemented its reputation as India's main computation centre, computing was also picking up at the Tata Institute of Fundamental Research (TIFR) in Bombay (now Mumbai). In 1960, the TIFR stole the ISI's computing thunder by building India's first indigenous digital computer, TIFRAC (Tata Institute of Fundamental Research Automatic Calculator).

## Building TIFRAC

Much like Mahalanobis, who coveted computers to process the massive amounts of data being collected by the National Sample Surveys, Homi Bhabha, the founding director of the TIFR and the Atomic Research Centre, coveted computers for nuclear energy projects.

Prime Minister Jawaharlal Nehru inspecting TIFRAC at the TIFR

In 1954, a group of physics postgraduates specializing in electronics began building India's first digital computer at the TIFR. Apart from Rangaswamy Narasimhan, who held a master's degree in electrical engineering from the California Institute of Technology, nobody else in the group had ever used a computer before! Technical information on making computers wasn't easily available, and the group had very limited knowledge to begin with. Still, they plodded on, reaching out to institutes in the US for technical inputs, importing major components and designing and tinkering around with a prototype. By 1959, their machine was ready and the following year, it was put to use.

The technology driving TIFRAC wasn't far behind what was being used elsewhere in the world during the 1950s, but in a fast-changing field, it had become obsolete by 1960. So, even though the computer was put to good use, Bhabha, like Mahalanobis, realized that India's technology gap would be difficult to fill with indigenous machines. He, too, desired a more powerful computer, bringing both scientists into a direct race. Although Mahalanobis had made great strides at the ISI, procuring two big computers from the UK and the Soviet Union, Bhabha surpassed him by acquiring CDC 3600, the largest commercially available computer at the time, for the TIFR in 1964, with a grant from the United States Agency for International Development. The addition of this machine catapulted the TIFR to the status of a national computing centre.

In the first year, the institute provided free computer time and programming help. It also conducted a number of programming courses to disseminate computing know-how and developed a variety of software packages. From academic institutions to businesses like banks and oil companies, the CDC had nearly 150 users in its first five years of operation. It propelled a growing interest in the commercial use of computers, and several companies began installing them in their offices, beginning with Esso Standard Eastern, a petroleum company in Mumbai.

## Growth of Computer Education

Engineering education in British India was largely rudimentary and designed to produce graduates who could work in railways, public works (such as road building) and irrigation (such as canal building). This barely met independent India's need for a technically qualified workforce for its diverse development projects. From Mahalanobis to Bhabha, all of India's leading scientists had to search feverishly for suitably qualified people who could work on the nation-building projects they were overseeing. They hired graduates from foreign universities and sent local graduates overseas for technical training.

Meanwhile, Prime Minister Jawaharlal Nehru set things in motion by opening the first Indian Institutes of Technology (IITs) during the 1950s and 1960s with foreign assistance. In August 1961, a consortium of top US universities, including the Massachusetts Institute of Technology, the California Institute of Technology and Princeton University, helped establish an IIT at Kanpur as a part of a decade-long programme called the Kanpur Indo-American Program (KIAP).

In the summer of 1963, under the KIAP, an IBM 1620 arrived at the premises of the fledgling institute. Back in the day, this computer was a novelty even at universities in North America and Europe. It was received at Kanpur by a team of foreign experts from the University of California, Berkeley, and Princeton University. Soon, IIT Kanpur began offering the first intensive short-term courses in computer basics and programming to academicians, researchers and industry managers. Thousands of people benefitted from these courses. By 1966, having acquired another IBM machine, IIT Kanpur became a hub of computer education and data processing activities.

Noticing that there were no textbooks or course materials, V. Rajaraman, a faculty member at the institute, wrote the first Indian textbooks on computing. These cheaply priced books were an instant hit and sold thousands of copies. In 1970, the institute began the first full-fledged postgraduate programme in computer science. Meanwhile, the other IITs also began building strong foundations in computer science and technology. However, in the absence of enough job opportunities in the field of computer science, most graduates ended up heading overseas for higher education and employment. So, even though institutes like the IITs had been founded with a view to strengthen India's technical workforce, they ended up becoming bases to export bright graduates overseas, mainly to the US.

This overseas connection though, became unexpectedly beneficial for India in the coming decades, as these graduates rose through the ranks at various technology companies, becoming international ambassadors of the skill and capabilities of Indian engineers. Many of them eventually tapped into Indian talent for the foreign companies they worked for and created more job opportunities in computing within India. This was a remarkable development that weathered some truly stormy conditions to transform a technologically backward country into a global hub of Information Technology (IT).

*As an electrical engineering student at IIT Madras in the 1970s, O.P. Agarwal belonged to the early generations of Indians exposed to advanced technology. He vividly recalls the first computer he laid eyes on: 'It was a giant machine full of blinking lights that needed an entire building for itself! But it was essentially an advanced calculator. We had to feed it with stacks of computer cards that made up a program (each card had a line of the program). The cards had to be punched using a card-punching machine, which was like a typewriter. If you made a mistake in typing even one alphabet in the entire program, the computer spewed out a message saying "Error".'*

*Having graduated from the institution with this memory, Agarwal wasn't prepared for his next encounter with the machine as a government official in the 1980s. 'The office boys had prepared a table saying that the computer would be kept on it. I laughed looking at it—there was no way a computer would fit there!'*

*The next day when the machine arrived, he promptly went to look at it. 'I thought the office had accidentally ordered a television instead of a computer!'*

### What Is Information Technology (IT)?

From hard drives and laptops to websites and messaging apps—IT encompasses all kinds of technologies used to create, store, exchange and use data.

## Stormy Times

The 1960s and 1970s were difficult decades for India. Wars, droughts and the rising price of oil took a massive toll on its treasury. Economic turmoil led to a rise in poverty and joblessness, increasing people's anger and disillusionment with the government. To quell the turmoil, the government began tightening its hold over the economy. Frugality became the order of the day to save India's depleting reserves of foreign exchange.

Even though computer education was spreading and business interest in computers had been growing during the 1960s and 1970s, these developments were happening away from the public eye. A vast majority of Indians continued to view machines like computers with suspicion. Workers feared that the new machines would take away their jobs. When the Mumbai office of the Life Insurance Corporation (LIC) installed a computer in 1963, violent protests broke out. By 1969, such protests had become so common that the government was forced to set up a committee to look into the matter.

This committee, headed by the economist Vinayak Mahadev Dandekar, acknowledged that computers would have no major impact on jobs in India. The use of computers was still extremely limited, and most companies used them mainly for number crunching. But given the general anxiety over computers leading to job loss, the committee suggested that before installing a computer, companies justified its purpose to their workers. This was a harsh proposal, but the government went ahead with it, placing a number of constraints on the use of computers in workplaces in India.

An unstated objective behind the government's restrictions, as journalist Dinesh C. Sharma reveals in his book on India's IT industry, was to control the influence of multinational companies, particularly IBM, which had entered India in 1951 and monopolized its computer market by 1970. IBM 1401 was the most popular computer in India during the 1970s, and the company leased it for a whopping 8,50,000 rupees annually! This amount included free maintenance and the services of an engineer who would assist clients with programming the machine to meet their specific needs. Indeed, IBM's service was top-notch and honed the programming skills of several Indian engineers. However, these were second-hand machines acquired from foreign markets, where they had become obsolete, and refurbished for Indian users.

This practice was neither unique to India nor to IBM. It was a norm prevailing in the computer industry at the time. The rate of obsolescence was extremely high in developed countries, so older models were abundantly available. Meanwhile, very few computers were being used in developing countries to justify the expense of setting up full-fledged manufacturing. Such conditions allowed IBM a good run of the Indian market with obsolete machines. However, trouble began towards the end of the 1960s.

To save scarce foreign exchange, the government had devalued the Indian rupee. This essentially meant that each dollar was now worth many more rupees. IBM was in luck—all its agreements were in US dollars, even though its clients in India paid the equivalent in rupees. Large payments to IBM caught the attention of the government auditor because government departments, ironically, were the company's biggest clients in India. This led to an investigation into the company's practices in India.

In the midst of this investigation, IBM applied for a license to market a new series of computers, the system/360. This time, though, the Indian government wasn't obliging. It asked IBM to slash prices of the computers, which would have become obsolete by the time they came to India, and delink the sale of its computers from servicing, allowing clients to service the machines on their own. It also ordered IBM to enter into a partnership with an Indian company.

For a company that had become used to setting its own terms in a technologically backward market, such orders were unpalatable. Meanwhile, the investigation into IBM's business practices revealed that it had been unfairly profiteering by 'dumping junk' and overcharging clients for it. In the face of this damning verdict, the company tried various means to protect its falling clout but eventually talks between IBM and the Indian government failed, and the company officially closed down its India operations in 1978. This was a bitter exit, which made news headlines not only in India but even overseas. Each side—the Indian government and IBM—blamed the other. Yet in the midst of this bitterness lay a big problem, and therein a big opportunity.

## A Blessing in Disguise

By the time IBM formally left India, it had hundreds of machines across the country. What was going to happen to these machines? Who would service them and supply spares when required? These were just some of the worries surrounding IBM's exit. During an interview with Sharma, O.P. Mehra, an IBM insider, revealed: 'IBM thought the Government of India machinery and the business and industry machinery would collapse if they walked out of India . . . All the railways were on IBM, steel plants were on IBM . . . airlines were on IBM, [a] substantial part of the LIC was on IBM, defence was considerably on IBM.

They thought that these machines would collapse, nobody would be able to maintain [them], and the government would come on their knees and say, "Okay, please stay".'

However, as Sharma goes on to write in his book, cracks had started appearing in IBM's monopoly even before its exit. In 1976, Ramesh Grover, an engineer who had serviced thirty-odd 1401s, quit IBM to form Computer Maintenance Services (CMS), which would maintain machines the company wasn't servicing. In light of IBM's exit, the government also set up its own maintenance company, Computer Maintenance Corporation (CMC), and ordered IBM to transfer its maintenance business, including stores housing thousands of spare components, to CMC. IBM's employees in India were given the option of joining CMC. Its other businesses in India were also acquired by companies such as International Data Management Limited (IDM), formed by former employees. In the end, worries about servicing and maintenance proved unfounded. Moreover, by ousting IBM, India had cut its dependence on obsolete computing technology and created an opportunity for indigenous companies to develop computers. But would they be able to fill the void?

On 8 August 1977, when IBM's imminent exit made front-page news in India, newspapers also carried advertisements for a new microcomputer, the 8C, developed by an Indian company—Hindustan Computers Limited (HCL)—that had been established the previous year. This was a coincidence, yet to readers, it appeared that HCL was the company the government had set up to replace IBM, and no one corrected this perception.

Indeed, news of IBM's exit had motivated a handful of Indian companies like Electronics Corporation of India Limited (ECIL), DCM Data Products and HCL to try and replace it.

With its inventive marketing and advertising strategies, HCL successfully attracted many first-time computer users. It also became the first Indian computer manufacturer to break into the overseas market when it ventured into Singapore and booked orders worth one million Singapore dollars for its microcomputer in 1980.

### What's in a Name?

DCM Data Products was India's oldest private computer manufacturer. But do you know what DCM stands for? Delhi Cloth Mills! That's because the company was originally a cloth maker. Similarly, the full form of Wipro is Western Indian Palm Refined Oil. And that's because it was originally in the business of oil.

Although Indian manufacturers soon filled the void left behind by IBM, Indian computers, like most other indigenous electronics, relied heavily on imported components (*also see pages 92–93*). During the 1970s, importing into India was a challenge because of the various restrictions imposed by the government. However, towards the end of the 1970s, especially in the wake of IBM's exit, the government began to rethink these restrictions.

## Winds of Change

Even though his mother Indira Gandhi was the prime minister of India, Rajiv Gandhi wasn't interested in politics. A technology buff, he liked to spend his time tinkering around with machines and flying aeroplanes. During the 1970s, Rajiv began working as a pilot in the UK, but life had other plans for him.

In 1980, when his younger brother Sanjay Gandhi was killed in an air crash, Rajiv returned to India to be by his mother's side. At the time, the country was preparing to host the 1982 Asian Games, and Rajiv was asked to join the organizing committee. Given his fascination with technology, he proposed computerizing various operations, such as guest coordination, athlete registration, compiling results and announcing medal tallies of the participating countries.

More than a hundred engineers from the National Informatics Centre (NIC), a government agency, were engaged in developing the software necessary for these tasks and connecting the eighteen stadiums hosting the games to a single network. This system enabled results to be accessed in real time and set a precedent for future games. Officials from the Seoul Olympics Committee came down to India to see it for themselves.

While working on the organizing committee, Rajiv came into close contact with N. Seshagiri, head of the NIC. Both shared a common interest in computers, and their connection paved the way for a landmark computer policy that was announced in November 1984, shortly after Rajiv Gandhi became India's prime minister following his mother's tragic death. The policy cut back government control over computers, encouraged private manufacturers and eased imports.

As importing became easier and cheaper, more computer manufacturers entered the market. Competition increased, and the price of computers fell. More people could now afford them, and personal computers entered Indian homes for the first time. The government also made a determined push to increase the visibility of these machines in India's public life and bridge the gap between computers and ordinary Indians. A major icebreaker was the computerization of ticket reservations in Indian Railways.

One of the largest railway networks in the world, Indian Railways was handling more than 40 lakh passengers travelling on thousands of different trains by 1984. It would receive around 50,000 reservation requests daily, for which passengers had to stand in long queues for hours on end as clerks juggled through numerous train ledgers to find the right one and jot down the reservation in it. If a seat wasn't available on the train being handled at a particular counter, passengers had to queue up again at the counter of an alternative train. This manual system was not only extremely cumbersome but also prone to errors and malpractices.

In 1984, CMC won a contract to computerize railway reservations. Within two years, this system was ready. It had been designed and implemented entirely by Indian engineers and was first launched in New Delhi. Fifty counters were opened at the booking office, and customers no longer had to wait for hours to make a reservation. They could head to any counter and book a reservation on any train. The job was done within minutes using computers. Cancelling tickets and getting refunds also became easier. Errors and malpractices reduced. The counter clerks were also happy because they no longer had to spend hours calculating the cash collected against tickets issued at the end of the day. Moreover, there was no reduction in staff. In fact, more counters had to be opened. The efficiency that computers introduced in the railway ticketing system was an eye-opener for both workers and the general public. It paved the way for public acceptance of computers in a country which had long mistrusted them as 'job-eating' machines.

Inspired by this success of the railways, other public services, such as banks, which had earlier opposed computerization, also adopted it. The government also started a large programme to introduce computers in schools (*also see page 184*). Such projects created a huge demand for computers. However, this growth could not be sustained.

Towards the end of the 1980s, India's economy began to falter again. Easing imports had drained foreign exchange, so import restrictions were reintroduced, and the government reduced its spending. Computer makers, who had been importing most of their components and relied on government demand, took a hit. A new decade was on the horizon, but it began with some deeply unsettling news—India barely had enough foreign exchange to buy three weeks' worth of imports! What would this mean for computing in India?

## Supercomputers

In a country where most people's livelihood relied on farming, accurate weather forecast was a pressing need. Apart from agriculture, weather forecasting would also provide warnings about extreme weather conditions, such as cyclones.

Since forecasting the weather in a large and geographically diverse country like India involved several complex calculations, the government decided to acquire a supercomputer for this. Back in the 1980s, this was a major technological leap, and India had to look overseas for a suitable machine. A supercomputer produced by the American manufacturer Cray was identified, but the US government refused to allow its export. It feared that India would use the supercomputer for military work instead of weather forecasting. The refusal angered Indian authorities, and in response, they established the Centre for Development of Advanced Computing (C-DAC), which built India's first supercomputer, PARAM 8000, in 1991. Since then, C-DAC has continued to make the PARAM series of supercomputers to meet India's increasing need for advanced computing, not just in agriculture but also in other fields such as space and defence.

*It was the early 1990s, and The Scindia School in Gwalior had just opened a brand-new science block, which housed a computer lab. It was a huge hit with students, though not entirely on account of the machines.*

*'It was the only fully air-conditioned room in the entire school,' Ankit Agrawal, a former student, cheekily confesses. He also admits to taking a fancy to the machines because they reminded him of* Star Trek, *the science fiction series he was hooked on to at the time. 'There were many computer engineers in the series, and in one episode, a character returns from the future and tries operating a computer by speaking to the hand-held mouse!'*

## Software Shows the Way

More than hardware, India's computing dreams have been built on software—the various applications or programs that allow computers to function.

The gradual spread of computing in India since the 1960s, helped an increasing number of Indians to unlock their skills in programming. As it turned out, these skills were highly sought after in the West, which had come to depend heavily on computers by the 1970s. This created an incredible window of opportunity, and some enterprising Indians were quick to seize it.

Among the early pioneers, as Sharma highlights in his book, was Narendra Patni, the son of a grain merchant from Agra, who opted out of the family business and headed to MIT in 1964 to pursue electrical engineering on a scholarship. Eventually, the young man developed an interest in publishing and began working for a publishing house in Massachusetts. In the early 1970s, the technology market in the West was shifting from bulky mainframe computers to smaller machines, and vast amounts of data needed to be shifted into the new systems. At the publishing company where Patni was working, this technological change meant that data, which had so far existed only as hard copies, had to be converted into tapes for the new machines.

This was a tedious manual exercise that would have been costly to complete in the US. But it struck Patni that he could have the conversion done in India for a fraction of the cost and then bring the tapes into the US. By October 1972, Patni had landed a deal. So, he founded a new company, Data Conversion Inc (DCI), and began sending tons of documents from Massachusetts to DCI's team of twenty-four data entry operators in Poona (now Pune).

Business boomed, and at its peak, DCI's team in India was converting hard copy data into tapes that stretched over eight kilometres, daily! Yet, the work wasn't without its problems. Tape readers were not readily available in India. After much persuasion, DCI was finally able to use the reader located at the Indian Meteorological Department in Delhi. But this complicated operations because converted tapes had to first make their way from Pune to Delhi, where they could be read to ensure accuracy before being sent to the US.

Patni realized that this complication could be solved if the data was fed directly into computers and then transferred to the tapes. However, for this to be possible, the necessary software had to be developed, and to develop the software, DCI needed more computers. So, Patni launched another company, Patni Computer Systems (PCS), to distribute minicomputers that were made by the American firm Data General, in India. No mere distributor, PCS was soon making use of Indian skills to create software for Data General's minicomputers. The business grew, and soon, the team expanded.

Heading PCS's software team was a gifted young programmer from IIT Kanpur—N.R. Narayana Murthy. Given the enormous scope of his work, Murthy hired other programmers for his team, which came to include many names—Nandan Mohan Nilekani, S. Gopalakrishnan, S.D. Shibulal, K. Dinesh, N.S. Raghavan, Ashok Arora—who would go on to leave a significant mark on independent India's technological history.

Armed with a team of talented programmers, PCS signed a record-breaking software deal worth 5,00,000 US dollars in 1979. In just a few years, Patni had successfully demonstrated how software offered a lucrative business opportunity for

India, and others were quick to latch on to the idea. In December 1980, Murthy resigned from PCS, followed shortly by his team. It was a shock exit, Sharma discloses, that left a bitter taste in Patni's mouth. But from this tumultuous episode emerged Infosys, one of India's biggest technology companies, founded by Murthy and his team from PCS.

The founding team of Infosys (L-R): N.R. Narayana Murthy, Nandan Mohan Nilekani, S. Gopalakrishnan, S.D. Shibulal, K. Dinesh, N.S. Raghavan, Ashok Arora

The software business in India began with labour-intensive work, such as data conversion, coding and debugging. Often, the only asset that fledgling software firms had was skill. Many of them didn't even have enough computers or basic infrastructure for their work. So, the best way to conduct business was to visit the offices of their clients and work on their machines. This type of work came to be known as 'body shopping', where clients paid for the workforce.

During the 1980s and thereafter, the computer industry benefited greatly from a change in the government's attitude. Instead of regulation and control, the government was increasingly seeking ways to make software exports take off. The computer policy of 1984 was a significant step in this direction. However, the government's greatest contribution was establishing Software Technology Parks (STPs), which offered a variety of incentives and crucial facilities to software firms.

In the absence of communication links between the US and India offices, most of the software being exported had to be physically transferred on floppy disks (a type of storage disk). The STPs eased this process by providing satellite links for seamless international communication and software transfers. At a time when the Internet was still not publicly available in India and one had to wait even to get a telephone connection, such workspaces were a groundbreaking step, as Sharma points out in his book *Indian Innovation, Not Jugaad,* and went a long way in making India the software giant it is today. The first STPs were established in Pune, Bangalore (now Bengaluru) and Bhubaneshwar in 1990. Many companies exporting software worth billions of dollars emerged in these STPs.

**>65**

the number of STPs in India in 2024

### India's Silicon Valley

During the 1970s, an area in Northern California, USA, became popular as 'Silicon Valley' because of the large number of technology companies based there. The moniker was inspired by the fact that most computer chips are made of silicon. By the late 1980s, another city in India was laying claim to this name—Bangalore (now Bengaluru).

At the time of Independence, Bengaluru—then a part of the kingdom of Mysore—was among the few cities in India with electricity and industries. The Wodeyars, who ruled the kingdom, encouraged a culture of innovation that continued to flourish even after Mysore became part of the Union of India. Some of India's earliest technical enterprises, such as Hindustan Aeronautics Limited, Bharat Electronics Limited and Bharat Heavy Electricals Limited, were founded in Bengaluru. During the 1970s, the city began cementing this legacy by earmarking land for building a technology cluster. By the 1980s, it was home to some of the biggest private technology companies in India, such as Infosys and Wipro, and it had also attracted the attention of international technology companies like Texas Instruments. The success of these firms inspired a vibrant start-up culture rooted in technology that turned Bengaluru into the undisputed tech capital of India.

## Computing for the World

The economic crisis of 1991 led to drastic reforms that changed India forever. For the first time since Independence, its markets were opened to the world (*also see pages 14–16*). Sharma corroborates how this encouraged many Western companies to set up software development facilities in India. As early as October 1992, Swissair—the national airline of Switzerland—set up Airline Financial Support Services (AFS) in collaboration with the Indian technology company Tata Consultancy Services (TCS). Connected to computers in Switzerland via satellite link, AFS handled various backend operations of the airline, especially accounting. By the late 1990s, it was also offering such services to other customers.

The success of AFS encouraged the development of a new industry in India—outsourcing—that handled backend operations for foreign clients swiftly and cheaply. While it depended on information and communication technology, the outsourcing industry catered to a variety of fields. Teams in India, for example, would do everything ranging from fixing software problems to filing income tax for customers overseas.

In 1998, outsourcing expanded to include call centres where English-speaking Indians would attend to customer calls for US businesses. Call centres increased the interaction between foreign customers and Indian workers, unleashing a cultural phenomenon that has made its way into many bestselling books and TV series.

The run-up to a new millennium that began in the year 2000 brought another major opportunity for computing in India in the form of the millennium bug.

How would you write the date 1 January 2000 in numerals? You would most probably write it as 01/01/2000, following the day/month/year format. But what if you could only put in the last two digits of the year? Then this date would go as 01/01/00 in numerals. Now, what's '00' supposed to mean, you might wonder . . . the beginning of time? This was precisely the trouble computers landed in during the run-up to the year 2000.

Most computers around the world had been programmed to read dates in the problematic 01/01/00 format, with just the last two digits of the year. If this wasn't corrected, computers could end up reading 01/01/2000 as 01/01/1900, and any computer activity that was programmed on a daily or yearly basis, such as flight records, would be flawed.

An army of Indian programmers was hired by foreign companies to scour through a massive number of computer programs and correct the date problem in each. Many Indian software companies earned huge revenues, grew bigger and found new customers in the process of doing this work. India's reputation for offering quality software services in a timely and cost-effective manner spread far and wide. Instead of 'job-eating' machines, computers came to be seen as 'job-creating' machines.

Together with growing government support and the public launch of the Internet in 1995, opportunities like the millennium bug proved to be a shot in the arm for Indian computing. The value of software exports increased dramatically, fuelling India's economic growth.

## An Ongoing Pursuit

From the spread of computer education and a growing population of Indians working and succeeding at technology companies overseas to the ingenuity of Indians who identified growth opportunities in the field and growing government support since the 1980s—India's success in computing has a variety of reasons.

Technology, however, is a fast-changing field, and as competition increases between firms within the country, as well as with other Asian countries, India needs to up its game. In a field that relies on human skill, it needs to invest more in developing a workforce equipped to handle higher-level tasks involving innovation, research and development. The quality of education needs to improve to keep pace with the industry.

Nevertheless, for a country that began its computing journey in the 1950s with hardly any resources and a public mistrust of computers, India has come a long way. Its success in establishing one of the world's most reputed computing industries is an extraordinary achievement—albeit one it needs to continue building on.

## The Simputer

In 2001, scientists at the Indian Institute of Science in Bengaluru developed the Simputer (Simple, Inexpensive, Multilingual People's Computer). Priced at 9,000 rupees, this handheld tablet was hailed for its numerous groundbreaking features, including applications in Indian languages, output in spoken language and an accelerometer to detect movement.

One of the most significant pieces of hardware developed in India, the *New York Times* called it 'computing as it would have looked if (Mahatma) Gandhi had invented it, then used Steve Jobs for his ad campaign.' However, lack of funding, marketing mettle and advanced hardware manufacturing in India meant that it never took off in a big way. Eventually, though, many of its features made their way into smartphones!

# 7

# Connecting India

Throughout history, humans have shared a need to connect and communicate thoughts, ideas and information with each other. They spoke to each other and eventually began sending letters, which led to the creation of postal systems. During the nineteenth century, communication was revolutionized by the telegraph and the telephone. The telegraph could quickly transmit messages in the form of Morse code—dots and dashes—while the telephone allowed people to speak to each other over ever-increasing distances.

Communication down the ages

## Morse Code

Want to have a bit of coding fun? Take a look at the Morse code here and try framing a message using it. What you will have at the end of this exercise is a message in one of the oldest electrical coding systems in the world.

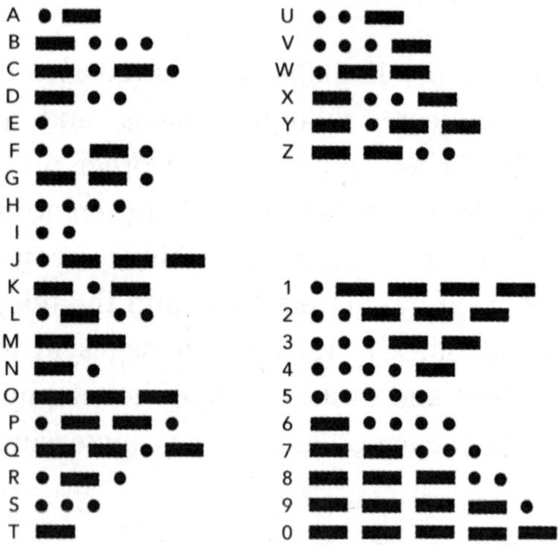

Source: https://students.cs.ucl.ac.uk/schoolslab/projects/PY2/introduction.html

Newly independent India had a postal service, telegraph and telephones, but these were largely restricted to urban places. The government needed to do more to improve the means of communication between different people and places in India. Boosting telecommunication—the electronic transmission of communication over long distances—was crucial.

### Make a Trip

In an era when letter writing was common, many people enjoyed stamp collecting or philately. The National Philatelic Museum in Delhi preserves this disappearing tradition with a collection of all commemorative stamps issued by the Government of India since 1947.

## Landlines Lead the Way

At the time of Independence, India had around 30 crore people and just one lakh telephones. By the early 1980s, these numbers stood at 80 crore people and 25 lakh telephones—that's just one telephone for every 280 people. Besides, many of these telephones were out of order. Connectivity in rural areas was particularly poor. Only three per cent of India's five lakh villages were on the telephone network. One man, however, was determined to change this.

Born in rural Orissa (now Odisha), Satyanarayan Gangaram Pitroda, also known as Sam Pitroda, had not seen or used a telephone till the age of twenty-two, but he possessed a keen interest in electronics. In the 1960s, with the support of friends and family, Pitroda made his way to the US to pursue electrical engineering at the

Sam Pitroda

Illinois Institute of Technology in Chicago. Eventually, Pitroda made a name for himself in the field of electronics, and as fate would have it, he became quite the expert in the technology behind telephone switches.

When you make a call on a telephone, the wires do not carry your voice directly to the listener. The call is routed through telephone switches that direct it towards the listener's telephone. The system is fairly straightforward, but what makes it mind-boggling is that a single switch is often connected to thousands of telephone lines and needs to direct the call towards the right telephone within milliseconds! That's not all, if the receiver's telephone is disconnected or busy, it needs to route this information back to the caller.

In the US, Pitroda became a multimillionaire developing advanced digital switches that went a long way in improving telephone connectivity. So, he was deeply troubled when he witnessed the poor state of telephone connectivity in India during a trip back home in 1980. It took years for people to install telephones at home, and even after the instrument would finally be installed, it would often go out of order because of the poor condition of telephone connectivity. The existing network, supported by several foreign companies, was clearly not working.

Pitroda decided that he had to do something to change this situation and his international credentials came in handy. In 1984, following a string of meetings, the Government of India approved his project—Centre for Development of Telematics (C-DOT)—to develop a suitable digital switch that would put countless Indian towns and villages on the telephone network for the very first time.

With a budget of 36 million US dollars and a deadline of 36 months, Pitroda went on a war footing to recruit a team of 200 Indian engineers for C-DOT. This team was going to develop switches that could handle high call volumes without consuming large amounts of electricity. But that wasn't all. The switches also had to be sturdy to withstand India's heat, humidity and dust without needing air-conditioning and regular maintenance. Ultimately, C-DOT developed different kinds of switches that could handle between 128 to 40,000 telephone lines for rural and urban India. In one go, the project modernized telephone connectivity in the country.

To popularize the technology behind these switches, C-DOT gave it away freely to private telephone operators instead of restricting it to the government network. This successfully countered pressure from various foreign companies selling their telephone switches in India. Pitroda wasn't done with his mission, though. To ensure that more people actually had access to telephones, he came up with the idea of opening Public Call Offices (PCOs) across the country. Introduced in the early 1990s, PCOs would have telephones connected to computerized meters that would record the length of a call and generate a bill accordingly. Twenty per cent of the bill would be retained by the owner of the PCO, and the rest would be paid to the telephone company. Shortly afterwards, PCOs with bright yellow signboards began sprouting up all over the country. They not only increased access to telephones but also became a source of livelihood for more than 20 lakh people. Moreover, the computerized meters exposed ordinary Indians to the benefits of computerization.

The times, however, were changing. A dire financial crisis in 1991 pushed India into a new economic era in which the government was no longer the big boss controlling its markets (*also see pages 14–15*). In 1994, telecommunication (or telecom), that had so far been dominated by the government, was opened up to private companies and services began to expand. But the future of the communication revolution ushered in by C-DOT-supported telephone lines, belonged elsewhere . . .

In many remote parts of India, PCOs became centres of social activity. People gathered to make and, sometimes, even receive calls! In some places, the PCO phone number became a community number, and managers would promptly dispatch runners to fetch the recipient of a call.

## Mobile Era

### How Does Your Mobile Phone Work?

What happens when you call someone using your mobile phone? Your voice is turned into a digital signal that travels through the air in the form of radio waves, which are picked up and turned back into a digital signal by a mobile tower near you. This signal is then sent to a mobile tower near the recipient either through a network of wires or cables or sometimes satellites.

The mobile tower near the recipient turns the signal into radio waves and transmits them to the recipient's mobile phone, which picks them up and turns them back into a digital signal and finally into sound.

The range of frequencies within which radio waves travel is called radio spectrum. A portion of this spectrum is allocated by the government for telecom. The terms 2G, 3G, 4G and 5G refer to different generations of mobile network technology. Mobile phones were launched in India on 2G. In 2008, 3G was introduced, followed by 4G in 2010 and 5G in 2022. With each generation, mobile networks in India have advanced, offering better connectivity to users. For example, 2G was primarily used for voice calls and had slow data speed. This improved significantly with 4G, which offered much faster data speed, allowing users to browse the Internet and watch videos more easily.

On 31 July 1995, Jyoti Basu, the chief minister of West Bengal, made the first mobile call in India. From his office in Calcutta (now Kolkata), he called and spoke to Sukh Ram, the communications minister based in Delhi. Although the call was made on a primitive mobile network using two boxy little Nokia phones, it signalled a service that would go on to connect India in a way landlines had never been able to.

Unlike fixed landlines, wireless mobile phones could be carried everywhere. They were also easier to procure—more models were available and one did not need too much paperwork to get a connection. However, like most new technologies, they were far too expensive and beyond the reach of most Indians.

During the 1990s, mobile handsets had to be imported into India and cost over 20,000 rupees. Meanwhile, mobile network operators charged more than eight rupees per minute for calls (both outgoing and incoming)! At the onset of the 2000s, the government reduced taxes on telecom technology, encouraging many new companies to join the market. As competition increased, mobile phones became cheaper and new features were introduced to lure buyers.

The Finnish company Nokia had dominated the Indian mobile phone market since the 1990s. In 2003, it launched Nokia 1100, the first 'made-for-India' mobile phone. Priced at 6,999 rupees, it was cheaper than previous models, had an anti-slip grip and came with an in-built radio, clock and torch to boot! In rural India, where electricity supply was irregular and power cuts were frequent, having a torch built into the mobile phone proved to be a terrific selling point. Moreover, the phone was so hardy and dust resistant that the first advertising campaign showed it attached to the grille of a truck to drive home the point! Soon after its release, the 1100 became one of the bestselling electronics of its time. Two years later, the American mobile maker Motorola rolled out the first made-in-India mobile, the C115. Priced at 1,700 rupees, it brought down mobile phone prices even more and encouraged local manufacturing.

Nokia 1100

Motorola C115

Although cheaper devices and newer features enticed many buyers, it was the drop in the calling rates that truly kickstarted the mobile revolution in India. The first major step in this direction was the 'calling-party-pays' system that made incoming calls free by 2004. Incidentally, this was also the year when the number of mobile phone connections surpassed landlines.

## The Missed Call

In the early years of mobile telephony when call charges were high, thrifty Indian users devised a clever way of delivering a message without paying a penny—the missed call! A missed call from a friend, family member or colleague could indicate messages like: 'I've arrived', 'call me back', etc. Enterprising marketers turned this into a popular marketing tool by encouraging people to make missed calls to receive pre-recorded content interspersed with advertisements. This ingenuity hit news headlines when ZipDial, a Bangalore-based missed call start-up, was taken over by the American social media company, Twitter (now called X).

Launched in 2009, ZipDial offered customers automated content, such as cricket match scores and Bollywood songs, in return for a missed call. In a time when the Internet was not as widely used, this service became extremely popular. Companies offering automated content through ZipDial also got to learn about customer preferences, which was useful for marketing their products.

By 2010, the mobile phone market in India was abounding in inexpensive smartphones, but what made these phones truly revolutionary was the world of Internet-enabled knowledge and services that they brought into the hands of crores of Indians for the very first time.

## The Internet Revolution

### How Does the Internet Work?

What happens when you log on to the Internet and search for information or browse websites? Your search request is converted into packets of information that travel through your connection to reach the network of the company providing you Internet services. This company is your Internet Service Provider (ISP). If you're using broadband, the data travels to your ISP through cables, and if you're using mobile data, it travels in the form of radio waves to a mobile tower near you, which sends it to the ISP. The ISP sends your data to a server that stores the information you are looking for. The server pulls out this information and sends it back to your ISP, which then sends it to your device through your Internet connection.

Simple as this sounds, it can be a rather thrilling operation! Sometimes, the server that hosts the information you're looking for, could be located in another corner of the world, and your data has to travel to it through a massive network of undersea fibre-optic Internet cables. Despite this, the Internet is able to throw up responses within milliseconds because your data is travelling at the speed of light—nearly three lakh kilometres per second. Put another way—the speed of your data can beat a rocket!

The Internet began in the 1960s as a network connecting different computers, allowing them to 'communicate' with each other. This meant that people working on computers in the network could use it to send files and data to each other. In the 1980s, Tim Berners-Lee, a talented computer programmer, had an incredible idea: what if this network of computers became a web of information that anyone who had access could tap into? This led Berners-Lee to create the World Wide Web (WWW). In 1993, the WWW was opened to the public, laying the ground for the Internet as we know it today.

The Internet, though, is older than the web. It came to India during the 1980s, when it was used to link computers at educational and research institutes in different parts of the country. This was called the Education and Research Network (ERNET). In 1995, the Internet was launched for the public, together with the mobile phone. Offered exclusively by the government-owned Videsh Sanchar Nigam Limited (VSNL), early connections were linked to telephone lines and only provided the Internet on computers. Known as dial-up connections, they were frustratingly slow and steeply priced. Users had to endure galling noises before the connection was established and wait several minutes for a web page to load (more, if the site had images, and let's not even mention videos). Moreover, you couldn't use the telephone if you were using the connection to browse the Internet. This 'service' would cost around 15,000 rupees for 250 hours and was only offered in major metro cities. Many early users mainly used it to send and receive e-mails—a novel application at the time.

### The Original 'Yahoo'

The late Bollywood actor Shammi Kapoor also happened to be a tech-lover and an early computer user. One of his lesser-known legacies is his role in popularizing the

Internet in India. In 1995, Kapoor became the face of the first Internet Users Club of India. He also created one of India's first personal websites–https://www.junglee.org.in/–an online memoir of his famous family. In 2000, when the web browser Yahoo! began its India network, yahoo.co.in, it invited Kapoor for the launch, where an orchestra broke into one of the actor's most iconic songs, 'Yahoo!', from his movie *Junglee*!

During the 1990s and early 2000s, most Indians owned neither a computer nor a landline. Besides, the astronomical charges meant that few people could afford using the Internet. To overcome the problem of limited access and affordability, Internet kiosks, also called cyber cafés, opened in different parts of the country. Much like PCOs, they allowed people to access the Internet publicly, at low rates. The first of these was the Coffee Day Cyber Café in Bangalore (now Bengaluru), which opened in 1995.

In 1998, VSNL's monopoly over the Internet was broken as the government allowed other firms to become ISPs in order to expand the reach of the Internet in India. The first of these ISPs was yet another government entity—the Mahanagar Telephone Nigam Limited (MTNL)—but soon private companies followed. As competition increased, the Internet infrastructure also began to grow and improve. By 2004, broadband services had been introduced in India. Instead of relying on telephone lines, they provided constant Internet access through cables and wireless devices. Broadband Internet became even faster when ISPs began using fibre-optic cables that carried data as light pulses instead of electric signals. In 2008, India had its first brush with hi-speed Internet on mobile phones when the 3G network was introduced. This was followed by 4G in 2010. However, mobile data was expensive, and even though scores of Indians had become mobile phone users by 2010, many of them could not afford to use the Internet on their mobile phones.

This changed in 2016, with the launch of Jio—a mobile network that offered free voice calls and unlimited 4G data to users. The 'free, free, free' campaign message worked wonders. Within six months, Jio had 10 crore users. Competing with its prices proved impossible, and many mobile network providers went out of business. Once the free trial period had captured enough customers, Jio introduced pricing. Yet, it remained highly affordable, and people continued with their subscriptions.

Apart from affordability, language was another obstacle in the spread of the Internet in India. The 'made-in-English' Internet had found one of its largest audiences among people who did not know the language well enough, and it needed to find a way to cater to them. Sensing an opportunity, websites like Webdunia pioneered the development of technology designed specifically to support Indian languages on the Internet and started offering multilingual content by the end of the 1990s. Eventually, tech giants like Google also began including Indian languages in their services. For example, Google Translate, that was launched in 2006, gradually began to translate English text into multiple Indian languages.

As Internet speed improved and usage rates fell, videos emerged as a popular form of language content. YouTube came to India in 2009 and by 2014, it had sixteen channels with more than 10 lakh Indian subscribers. Many of these channels offered content in Indian languages. In fact, one of the largest YouTube channels in the world belongs to T-Series, an Indian music label and movie studio that primarily carries content in Hindi and other regional languages.

In a country where many people could not read or write, access to the Internet was made even easier with the coming of voice-recognition software, such as Apple's virtual assistant Siri that was launched in 2011 (*also see page 230*). Eventually, these AI-based assistants learned to understand Indian languages, and users who had difficulties reading and typing could simply command their phone by speaking to it! By 2017, Google was reporting an exponential increase in voice-based search inquiries in Indian languages.

## Indians and the Internet

**>80 crore**

active Internet users, more than 80% of whom access it on their mobile phones

**54%**

of Internet users are from rural India

**98 minutes**

the average time users spend on the Internet daily

Source: The Internet and Mobile Association of India (IAMAI), 'Internet in India Report 2023.'

## Men vs Women

**54%**
Male users

**46%**
Female users

## Top Activities on the Internet

**86%:** Watching videos
**76%:** Communication, for example WhatsApp messages, emails and video calls
**70%:** Using social media
**53%:** Online gaming
**52%:** Online shopping
**45%:** Digital payments on apps such as UPI
**3%:** Online learning

## Languages of the Internet

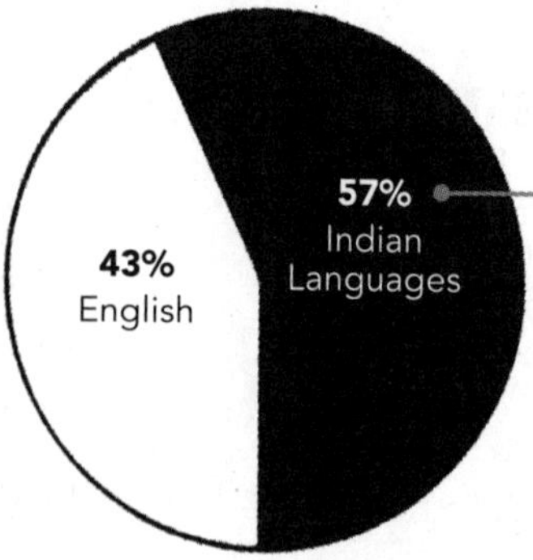


- **24%** Hindi
- **3%** Marathi
- **6%** Tamil
- **3%** Gujarati
- **4%** Telugu
- **2%** Bengali
- **2%** Kannada
- **3%** Malayalam
- **10%** Others

## Big Opportunity, Big Challenges

When you use the Internet, you immerse yourself in a different world, also called cyberspace. It's an exciting place, full of possibilities. In the beginning, the Internet mainly had websites offering information about a variety of things happening globally. It also allowed users to connect with each other through email and chat. As the years progressed, users could do more and more using the Internet. They could access a greater variety of content, including digital magazines, newspapers, books, songs and movies. They could connect with others in more ways, most notably through social media. They could shop online, bank online, learn online, book taxis online . . . As the Internet grew, so did the choices it offered. No matter where you were, if you had Internet access, the world, quite literally, was just a click away.

Slowly, the Internet became a way of life for crores of Indians. Surveys reported that many people felt the Internet had improved their lives, especially by allowing them to entertain themselves and connect with others. Yet not everything was quite right about this world. Much like the real world, even cyberspace had troublemakers lurking within it.

### Some Forms of Internet Misuse

**Stealing money:** Scamming users through various means, such as false communication, to steal money online

**Cyber bullying:** Harassing users by trolling them, sending threats, etc.

**Spreading disinformation:** Circulating fake news online

**Cyber warfare:** Using the Internet to attack other countries, for example hacking into and damaging their critical digital systems, such as those used for banking or by the military

In 1998, shortly after India declared itself a nuclear-weapons state, hackers broke into the computer system at the Bhabha Atomic Research Centre using the Internet and gained access to private emails and files. They made the nuclear facility vulnerable to several other attackers. Things could have gone terribly wrong except those were still early days and the hackers, according to some media reports, were just a group of disgruntled American youth who were upset with India when they heard of its top-secret nuclear tests (*also see page 43*) and simply wanted to vent their frustration! Even though this remains a contested fact, the incident was an indication of the dangers posed by the Internet. Hiding behind its cover were faceless users capable of hatching and implementing all kinds of sinister plans, and the more people used the Internet, the more likely they were to fall prey to such crimes.

Alarmed by the misuse of technology, the government passed the Information Technology (IT) Act in 2000, which included the first set of laws against cybercrime (*also see page 174*). In 2018, the government also launched the Indian Cyber Crime Coordination Centre (I4C), which includes initiatives such as:

- the National Cyber Crime Reporting Portal (https://cybercrime.gov.in), with a special focus on crimes against women and children;
- a Citizen Financial Cyber Fraud Reporting and Management System to stop fraudsters from stealing money online. This system has reportedly saved more than 1,200 crore rupees in more than 4.7 lakh complaints;
- a hotline number, 1930, for cyber complaints;
- National Cyber Forensic Laboratories to assist police investigation, for example, by checking mobile and computer records;
- courses to educate officials on various aspects of cybercrime;
- and regular publicity through social media, radio, newspapers and text messages to raise public awareness against cybercrime.

Despite initiatives to alert citizens and battle cybercrime, criminal activities online have continued to increase. According to the National Crime Records Bureau, India recorded more than 65,000 cybercrime cases in 2022, compared to 52,974 cases in 2021. In the fast-changing world of technology, keeping up with wrongdoers has proved to be a challenge for countries everywhere. Misuse of the Internet, however, is not restricted to crimes online. It can also unleash mayhem in the real world. In India, disinformation or fake news has been particularly troublesome, leading to many widely reported cases of violence against individuals and communities.

In September 2015, Mohammad Akhlaq was beaten to death by a group of people holding extreme views on cow protection after fake images circulated on social media showed that he had been storing beef in his house. Similarly, in May 2017, fake news on social media about a group of strangers kidnapping children fanned unrest and sparked violence in Jharkhand. Seven people were murdered by enraged mobs that did not bother to confirm the truth before resorting to such extreme actions.

Hundreds of such cases have been reported in the Indian media, prompting action by social media platforms as well as informed citizens. For example, websites like Alt News and SM Hoax Slayer have been created to fact-check fake news. Meanwhile, in the aftermath of the 2017 mob violence in Jharkhand, WhatsApp—that has been widely used to spread fake news—began limiting forwards.

Have you ever wondered how technology companies like Google and Facebook that offer free services through the Internet have become some of the richest companies in the world? This has happened mainly because they have managed to attract an overwhelming majority of Internet users. More than 37 crore Indians were using Facebook in 2024 and nearly 90 per cent used Google's search engine. How does this translate into money? Largely through advertising. Seems fine, doesn't it? After all, don't we see advertisements everywhere? In newspapers, on billboards, while listening to the radio. But advertisements on the Internet are far more targeted because Internet companies are using software that is getting better and better at understanding the tastes and preferences of users by tracking their online activities. For example, if you regularly order food and keep looking up new dishes, restaurants and cuisines online, you are likely to find advertisements related to food and dining while surfing the Internet. This makes many people worry about their privacy online.

But that's not all. As many books and documentaries have shown, Internet platforms often go to great lengths to retain the attention of users, making it an extremely addictive media. In recent years, many founders of technology companies have also acknowledged this problem. During a speech in November 2017, Facebook's founding president Sean Parker said that the social networking site aimed to capture as much time and attention of its users as possible. It was this mindset that led it to create the 'like' button. The prospect of receiving likes on their posts would encourage users to keep posting new content:

> 'It literally changes your relationship with society, with each other. It probably interferes with productivity in weird ways. God only knows what it's doing to our children's brains.'

Different studies have found growing rates of Internet addiction among students and young professionals, especially in urban India. Participants suffering from addiction reported feeling restless when they did not have Internet access, waking up from their sleep to check notifications on their mobile phones, sleeping late because they were online and neglecting studies and other activities to spend time on the Internet, particularly on social media. Naturally, this had a negative effect on their mental health.

They slept poorly and found it hard to concentrate on their work. Many of them found face-to-face interactions and emotional bonding challenging.

This is not a new problem. Neither is it unique to India. Like most Internet-based problems, it is shared by countries around the world. China has identified Internet-addiction as a serious health crisis, and South Korea has hundreds of tech de-addiction centres. In India, the first Internet de-addiction centre called Service for Healthy Use of Technology (SHUT) opened in Bengaluru in April 2014. In July, another such centre was started by the Uday Foundation in Delhi.

**>5 hours**

American psychologist Jean Twenge says that teenagers who spend over five hours on social media in a day are far more likely to report feeling depressed.

## No Easy Answers

Although Internet use has increased dramatically in India, most users are still new to it and have little to no training on how to utilize it in productive ways. Many also lack adequate awareness to save themselves from online scams and fake news. Even though the government has made a massive push to connect India through the spread of telecom, and taken steps to control cybercrime, it needs to do more to prepare ordinary Indians for the onslaught of new technologies in their lives.

## Saving the Internet

Is social media the Internet, or is it part of the Internet? If you think that's a dumb question, think again. In October 2014, Mark Zuckerberg, the famous founder of Facebook flew down to India with a proposal called Internet.org (it was eventually called Free Basics), under which his company was offering 'free Internet' to Indians. The proposal seemed enticing, but something was off about it, and Internet activists were quick to catch on.

Facebook wasn't offering the World Wide Web. What it was offering was more like Facebook's web, where users would have free access to a handful of websites, including Facebook, but not the entire Internet. Allowing such a proposal would go against the idea of net neutrality—the principle that ISPs should treat all websites equally. This means they should not favour some websites by slowing down, blocking or charging more money to access others.

Incidentally, around the time Facebook came to India with this proposal, the activists were already arguing with ISPs about net neutrality, and the Telecom Regulatory Authority of India (TRAI), which controls such issues, had put out a notice that it would relook at the principle of net neutrality. Despite this, Facebook went ahead and launched Internet.org.

Agitated by this, a group of Internet activists led by journalist Nikhil Pahwa launched 'Save the Internet', a historic campaign that pitted them against none other than Mark Zuckerberg and Facebook. While Pahwa and his supporters worked with a group of comedians to put out a hilarious viral video that simplified and popularized the idea of net neutrality, Facebook started pressuring the Indian government and warned its users that TRAI could ban its plans to give free Internet to Indians if net neutrality was upheld. In the end, though, the activists won. TRAI upheld net neutrality, and Facebook had to withdraw its grand scheme. Eventually, the 'Save the Internet' campaign led to the creation of the Internet Freedom Foundation, a non-profit organization that works to protect and promote the digital rights of Internet users in India, in 2016.

# PART 2

# POWERING PEOPLE

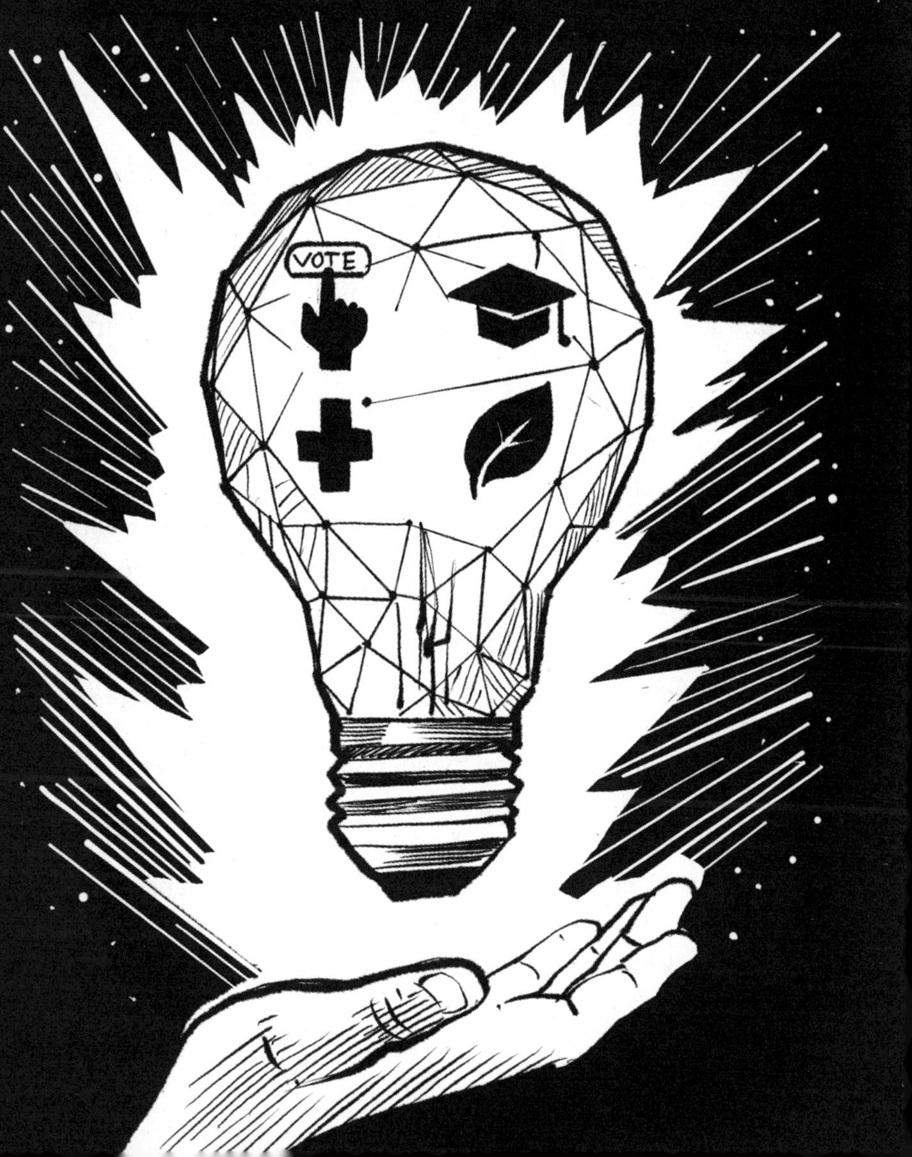

# 8

# Democracy and Technology

Newly independent India was a deeply divided land. People were separated by caste—social groups into which they were born—which historically determined the work they did. There was also massive economic inequality: while some people had plenty of money, most found it hard to afford even two meals a day. Those from the so-called lower castes, who had long been forced into low-paying menial jobs, were among the poorest. Cutting across these divisions was gender. Seen as breadwinners, men were usually considered superior to women, and female infanticide (killing newborn baby girls) was common in many places. To make matters worse, at the time of Independence, the land was partitioned to create Muslim-majority Pakistan and Hindu-majority India, intensifying religious tensions. What could possibly unify such a divided population?

For the leaders of independent India, an answer to this dilemma lay in democracy—empowering all Indians above a certain age, regardless of their differences, with the right to vote and elect a government that would be answerable to them. In the years since Independence, rapidly advancing technology has had a profound impact on democracy in India.

From the very act of voting to the ways in which governments engage with citizens, it has transformed Indian politics.

## Voting Technology

Through much of history, the right to vote had been considered a privilege, usually restricted to men with power and property. In many parts of the world people struggled long and hard to win voting rights. In the US, for example, women were not allowed to vote until 1920, while in Australia, indigenous people only began voting from 1962. So, when newly independent India gave its largely impoverished and uneducated people the right to vote, many called this the greatest experiment in democracy the world had ever seen.

On 25 January 1950, India established its first Election Commission, which worked tirelessly to get the country election-ready. One of the many important things the commission deliberated on was the process of voting—it had to be easy enough for everyone to understand.

Initially, at the polling booths, each party was allotted a ballot box bearing its symbol, and voters simply had to drop their ballot paper into the box bearing the symbol of the party they wanted to vote for. In 1962, this system was changed. Voters now needed to stamp on the party symbol of their chosen candidate on the ballot paper before dropping it into a common ballot box.

Free and fair elections—where people are able to vote for a political party of their choice without any pressure, and where every vote counts—form the basis of democracy. But as the number of voters and political parties increased over the years, competition for votes intensified. Political parties began to spend large sums of money on their campaigns to

A voter inserting his ballot paper into a box bearing the symbol of the political party he favours during the first General Elections held in India in 1951.

woo voters. With so much money being spent on election campaigns, the pressure to win increased significantly, leading to growing complaints of wrongdoing.

In many places, armed individuals would capture polling booths, stuffing the common ballot box with votes for the party they supported, and coercing other voters to vote for it. Sometimes, the result of an election would be changed by producing a false record of the number of the votes won by a party. Booth capturing and vote rigging were undermining elections, and the Election Commission wondered how to tackle the menace. Apart from such misconduct, the use of ballot papers was extremely tedious and time-consuming as crores of papers had to be printed, transported to polling booths, stored safely and counted manually. The steel ballot boxes also needed regular maintenance to prevent them from corroding.

During the 1970s, the Election Commission asked the Electronics Corporation of India (ECIL) to design a voting machine that would do away with ballot papers. Without ballot papers, it was possible to address the danger of illegally stuffing ballot boxes and wrongly counting votes. By 1979, ECIL had developed a working model of an Electronic Voting Machine (EVM), and the following year, the commission demonstrated it to representatives from various political parties. In June 1981, the government also approved an EVM design submitted by Bharat Electronics Limited (BEL), and both ECIL and BEL began manufacturing EVMs for Indian elections.

EVMs were first used in an election held at Paravur in Kerala in 1982. However, they had been used without obtaining the necessary permission and the losing candidate, A.C. Jose, challenged the election verdict in the Supreme Court. In 1984, the court struck down the election, even though it refrained from commenting on the advantages and disadvantages of using EVMs. The case made it clear that EVMs could not be used unless there was a law in place that permitted their use, and this was precisely what happened in 1989.

But before that, in 1988, two professors from IIT Bombay, A.G. Rao and Ravi Poovaiah, were roped in to improve the crude and bulky design of the existing EVM. Using sturdy materials like engineering plastics, they created a durable, low-cost, lightweight, portable machine with programming instructions hardwired into its circuit board.

Each EVM was a standalone unit, not connected to any central network. This protected the machine from hacking attempts. To bolster security, the electronic sealing of the machine was topped with traditional sealing wax, so, any attempt to tamper with it would leave a visible proof. Another key feature of the new EVM was that it only allowed five votes per minute. This slowed the pace of voting to curtail the probability of false ballots.

In March 1989, Rao and Poovaiah's design was accepted by both ECIL and BEL, and the companies rushed to manufacture EVMs in time for the elections. However, many political parties continued to worry that EVMs could be manipulated to produce an incorrect result. So, the Election Commission had to put the machines on hold.

In January 1990, the government set up the Electoral Reforms Committee, a team of technical experts that put EVMs through extensive technical tests, including a mock election. After conducting these tests, the committee confirmed that EVMs were technically sound, secure and transparent and should be put to use without further delay. This was followed by discussions with various political parties, and in 1998, EVMs were back in action. The use of EVMs increased thereafter and in the 2004 general elections, they replaced ballot papers all across the country. Even as India embraced electronic voting, many countries around the world, such as England, France, the US and the Netherlands, began banning it because of alleged issues in the software, which made it vulnerable to errors. This fanned doubts over the technology—were EVMs recording votes correctly?

To address this issue, in 2013, the Supreme Court ruled that EVMs had to produce a physical proof—a Voter Verifiable Paper Audit Trail (VVPAT)—to confirm that votes had been recorded correctly. EVMs equipped to produce a VVPAT replaced the old machines in 2017. Nevertheless, suspicions continued, and in 2021, the Citizens' Commission on Elections, a civil society organization, released a report questioning the inner workings of EVMs.

From the time they were introduced, EVMs have been constantly challenged. Although the Supreme Court eventually refused to entertain any request for reverting to ballot papers, it has often made recommendations such as the addition of VVPATs, to address suspicions around EVMs.

Besides, in the world's most populous democracy, EVMs have played an important role in saving paper as well as expenses incurred on storage, transportation, counting and security of ballot papers. Some researchers suggest that EVMs have simplified the voting process for vulnerable citizens. Uneducated or disabled voters, for example, have found it easier to press a button on the EVM instead of making a mark on a paper ballot in a multiparty election. The ease of voting has only been matched by the ease of counting votes as polling officers no longer need to struggle with unclear marks on paper ballots. Counting has become faster and more efficient, making it possible to declare the results sooner. Researchers have also found that using EVMs has led to a decline in booth capturing and vote rigging, although it hasn't been able to address poll violence and attempts to bribe or coerce voters into voting for a particular party. Moreover, India-made EVMs have also been exported to countries like Bhutan, Nepal and Namibia.

## Electronic Voting Machine

The EVM is a machine that counts votes. It is powered by a battery and has an expected shelf-life of fifteen years.

- One hundred and eighty days prior to polling: EVMs dispatched to the states and tracked using GPS-based software.
- Three weeks before polling: assigned to constituencies.
- Two weeks before polling: assigned to polling booths, at random.
- On polling day, a mock poll of at least fifty votes is conducted in each polling station, and the EVM and VVPAT tallies are compared in presence of the polling agents.
- After polling is over, the complete EVM unit is sealed and sent to storage rooms, where they are guarded by the Central Reserve Police Force. Representatives of the candidates are allowed to follow the vehicle that carries the EVMs to the storage rooms, and candidates are allowed to put their own seals on the storage room.

### Balloting Unit

**Ballot list** with the names of the candidates and their party symbols is fixed on the balloting unit after the last date for candidate withdrawal. Typically, a balloting unit has space for sixteen entries. If there are more, additional units are required.

**Candidate button** corresponding to the name on the ballot list. Every time it is pressed, the choice is transmitted to the control unit, where it is stored.

**Candidate lamp** lights up when the corresponding candidate button is pressed.

### VVPAT

Paper slip bearing the symbol, name and serial number of the candidate chosen by a voter is printed by the VVPAT and is visible for seven seconds in the **viewing window**, after which it drops into a secure box.

### Control Unit

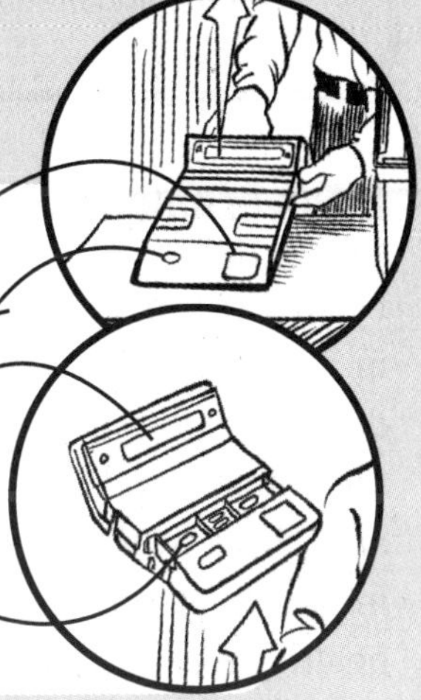

**Ballot button**: A voter can only cast a vote when the polling officer presses this button.

**Total button** gives the total number of votes polled.

**Display section** where totals are displayed.

**Close button**: Once polling is over, the presiding officer presses this button inside the control unit. No votes can be cast after this.

Source: 'Explained: India's New Proposal for Migrant Voting,' *The Hindu* and Citizens Commission on Elections Report on EVMs and VVPAT, 2021.

### Cambridge Analytica

Can technology be used to sway voters and influence election results? One of the biggest global scandals involving such misuse of technology came to light in 2018, when media reports revealed how Cambridge Analytica, a British company working with political parties, illegally collected the data of lakhs of Facebook users to understand their voting preferences and tailored ads that would influence their voting behaviour. It allegedly used these tactics to shape public opinion in favour of the UK leaving the European Union and to win support for Donald Trump's US presidential campaign in 2016. The reports also revealed how the company had used these tactics in other countries, including India, where it had allegedly accessed the data of more than five lakh people. However, no concrete evidence emerged to suggest that Indian elections had been manipulated.

## E-Government

From birth to death, the government plays an important role in a citizen's life. Government authorities register births and deaths. They issue passports that allow citizens to travel outside the country and licences that allow them to conduct business and drive within the country. The government plans and implements various welfare schemes that deliver affordable healthcare, education, food and employment to the citizens and provides them documents to avail of such schemes. It also collects taxes that help it to run the country.

Till the 2000s, these functions usually involved extensive physical interactions between government employees and citizens. In a large and populous country, this wasn't always convenient. Sometimes, people had to travel long distances to reach a government office to meet the officials. At times, unscrupulous government employees would demand bribes to do their work.

During the 2000s, as electricity spread across the country and more people gained access to computers, mobile phones and the Internet, many government services such as filing taxes began to be offered online. This reduced crowds at government offices, deterred corruption and made government services faster and more transparent. In May 2006, India launched its first National e-Governance Plan that actively promoted the use of technology to deliver various government services to citizens. One of the greatest technological leaps in e-governance began with the introduction of Aadhaar, the world's largest identity project.

*During the 1980s, when Rajiv Gandhi became India's prime minister, computers were still uncommon in the country, and most ministers and top government officials did not know much about them. So, when Rajiv Gandhi initiated the use of computers in government offices, it led to some amusing incidents. In his memoir,* Backstage: The Story Behind India's High Growth Years, *economist Montek Singh Ahluwalia recounts how the railway minister unspooled a large sheet of paper across the prime minister's desk when he was asked to put data on a 'spreadsheet'!*

## Identity Matters

India is home to crores of people. To serve them, the government first needs to identify them. How does the government identify so many people? By issuing various identity cards and documents, such as voter IDs, ration cards, driving licences and passports. Despite this, successive governments faced difficulties in effectively identifying all Indians. This was happening because many people didn't have documentary evidence, such as a birth certificate or an address proof, that was necessary to get these IDs and documents, which helped the government identify them. For example, many people didn't have a birth certificate because their birth had not been registered. Some didn't even know their birthdays! Many didn't have any address proof because they moved around the country for work or were too poor to afford to live in a house.

In the absence of such identification, the government found that its welfare schemes often failed to reach people in need. Instead, much of its aid was either getting wasted or illegally diverted to benefit others. In 1985, Prime Minister Rajiv Gandhi revealed that for every rupee that the government spent on welfare, only fifteen paise reached those in need!

By 2000, India's population had crossed 100 crores, and the country was facing an identity crisis. Unless this was resolved, welfare schemes would continue to suffer, impacting the trust of voters and the political future of elected parties. The government needed to find a reliable way to identify people, and that's how the idea of Aadhaar was born.

Unlike other IDs, Aadhaar relied on biometrics—eye scans and fingerprints—that are unique to every person and which a majority could submit easily. Although Aadhaar enrolment also required people to submit other identity proofs they possessed, it did not depend entirely on these. People who did not possess such documents could get a certificate ascertaining their identity from an 'introducer'—a government official or community leader who could verify their existence.

The idea of a biometrics-based national identity card had been floating around for a few years, but it was finally introduced by the United Progressive Alliance (UPA) led by the Congress party in 2008–2009. The UPA set up the Unique Identification Authority of India (UIDAI) in January 2009 and invited Nandan Nilekani—who had been the chairman of the hugely successful Indian technology company Infosys—to lead it. The ID cards issued under this project were named *Aadhaar*, which means 'foundation' in Hindi and a few other Indian languages.

Aadhaar sought to provide every citizen of India with a twelve-digit unique identification number based on biometric data, which would eliminate duplication and fake entries in government records. In a country with more than 100 crore people, this was a gigantic technological undertaking. The relatively small team led by Nilekani had to create software that could confirm the uniqueness of the biometric data collected from every single person after checking it against crores of others and then assign it an exclusive twelve-digit number. Despite this daunting challenge, the team worked at an extraordinary speed, and on 29 September 2010, thirty-year-old Ranjana Sonawane from Tembhli, a tribal village in Maharashtra, became the first person to get an Aadhaar number.

In 2010, the government had also presented a draft National Identification Authority Bill before the Parliament, to give Aadhaar a legal status and greater authority. However, even though Aadhaar enrolments continued, the bill was rejected by the parliament. The ground had been laid for one of the biggest challenges facing the project—privacy. How had the government allowed UIDAI to collect sensitive biometric data, unique and personal to every individual, along with other information, without any law that would ensure its protection and prevent misuse?

Following the rejection, the bill was withdrawn and the UPA did not revise and take it back for reconsideration. Moreover, in the general elections of 2014 it was voted out of power and replaced by the Bhartiya Janata Party (BJP) that had publicly opposed Aadhaar. The fate of the project looked uncertain. But contrary to general expectation, the BJP put its full political might behind Aadhaar and scaled it up.

Aadhaar had been originally envisioned as a way of identifying those in need and delivering welfare schemes to them. Among its earliest applications was changing the way government discounts on cooking gas cylinders were delivered to households. Many Indian households use cooking gas to prepare food, but cooking-gas cylinders are expensive. So, the government would fix a discounted rate (subsidy) for them. For example, if the cost of a cylinder was 800 rupees, the government would fix the price at 600 rupees. Gas companies were instructed to sell the cylinders to customers for household use at this price, and the remaining 200 rupees would be paid to the companies by the government. But this system was leaky. Some sellers, for example, would take the money from the government but would sell the discounted cylinders meant for households to businesses at the market price, thereby earning a neat profit. This also led to a general shortfall of cylinders for household use. Under the new scheme, the government fixed the number of subsidized cylinders households could get each year, and instead of paying the gas companies, it transferred the discount (200 rupees) directly to the Aadhaar-linked bank accounts of customers. The customers in turn were to buy the cylinders from the companies at the market price (800 rupees).

Not only did the BJP scale up such cash transfer schemes—also called Direct Benefit Transfer (DBT)—nationwide, but it also widened their scope to include various other government subsidies and pensions. However, its first grand expansion was the Pradhan Mantri Jan Dhan Yojana (prime minister's people's money scheme) launched in August 2014.

When the BJP came to power in 2014, more than 70 crore Indians (over half the population at that time) had an Aadhaar number, but most of them did not have a bank account. Without a bank account, cash transfer schemes would not work. Under the Jan Dhan Yojana, every Indian in need of government aid could open a zero-balance, Aadhaar-linked bank account. This would get them a debit card to withdraw money and an insurance of one lakh rupees in case of any personal crisis. A record-breaking 1.8 crore Jan Dhan accounts were opened shortly after the scheme was announced, introducing a large number of Indians to banking for the very first time.

Boosting this expansion was the mobile revolution. By 2014, crores of Indians were using mobile phones and the cost of mobile data, which allowed users to access the Internet on the mobile phone, was also reducing. In 2015, the BJP government announced the Digital India Campaign to improve Internet connectivity in the country and offer more government services online. The very next year, Reliance Industries launched Jio, a network that offered mobile data at throwaway prices, turning crores of Indians into Internet users almost instantly. Meanwhile, the government pushed an Aadhaar Act through the Parliament, finally giving the project legal recognition. Under the Act, any individual who had been residing in India continuously for 182 days was eligible to apply for Aadhaar.

Aadhaar, Jan Dhan and expanding mobile data usage, together known as JAM (Jan Dhan, Aadhaar, Mobiles), laid the ground for India Stack—a set of government-backed digital tools that allowed people to do a number of things online, such as sign documents (eSign) and store copies of important identity proofs and other documents in a digital locker (DigiLocker). One of the most popular digital tools developed under India Stack was the Unified Payments Interface (UPI). It enabled people to transfer money to each other using their mobile phones.

The use of UPI ballooned towards the end of 2016 when the government declared that existing 500- and 1000-rupee notes could no longer be used as currency. This decision, also called demonetization, made India go cashless almost overnight because these notes accounted for more than 85 per cent of the country's cash. Even though many people were deeply distressed by it, demonetization popularized digital payments. This trend continued during the COVID-19 pandemic that began in 2020, as most people opted for contactless digital payments to avoid contracting the infection. Payments made through UPI increased from 92 crores in 2017–2018 to 13,116 crores in 2023–2024!

Since June 2023, India has also signed agreements with several different nations, such as Armenia, Antigua and Barbuda, to share India Stack. Meanwhile, countries such as Singapore and France have begun accepting UPI payments.

## The Battle for Privacy

Even as India, once considered technologically backward, was dazzling the world with its advanced digital infrastructure, worries around privacy had grown bigger. Aadhaar now lay at the centre of the massive digital infrastructure the government had created, and Indians had to share biometric data for everything, from getting SIM cards for mobile phones to opening bank accounts, obtaining driving licences and enrolling for all-India exams. Many people expressed fears that this data could be easily exploited for mass surveillance—secretly tracking people's lives—by monitoring their Aadhaar-based activities. There were also doubts around the safety of the central digital database that recorded the data of all Aadhaar holders. What if someone hacked into it and illegally gained access to this data? Such fears deepened in 2018 when media reports stated that the database had indeed been breached, compromising the data of crores of Aadhaar holders.

Quite apart from privacy and data breaches, disturbing reports were pouring in about how the technology-driven system had excluded many people from accessing government services. Disabled people, for example, reported not being able to get their disability pension because of problems in registering their biometric data. Other reports spoke of people dying of hunger because their ration card had not been linked to Aadhaar or because their Aadhaar number had been linked to another bank account, and they had not received cash transfers.

In 2018, all these issues landed up before the Supreme Court. The case was led by K.S. Puttaswamy, a retired judge of the Karnataka High Court. In 2017, a team of lawyers under him had successfully argued that privacy was a fundamental right. Although the Supreme Court had accepted their argument, it clarified that the right to privacy, like all fundamental rights, wasn't absolute. People were entitled to protect their personal information, so long as they were not using this to hide wrongdoings that could hurt other people or the country. For example, a criminal could not withhold personal information from the police claiming the right to privacy.

Now, Puttaswamy and several others who opposed Aadhaar stood before the court alleging that by collecting personal biometric data and linking it to many different schemes and services, the government was violating the right to privacy. For thirty-eight days, between 17 January and 10 May 2018, five judges of the Supreme Court heard a series of arguments, for and against Aadhaar. Then, they went back to deliberate and decide. By September, the court had a decision—Aadhaar would stay but with restrictions. It had originally been conceived as a way of delivering welfare benefits directly to the needy, and that's what it should essentially be. While reading out its verdict the court said:

> 'The Constitution does not permit the establishment of an authority that . . . can chain every Indian citizen/resident to a central data bank and maintain lifelong records and logs of that individual.'

### The Aadhaar Verdict

Aadhaar is unique and more foolproof than other identification documents because it's based on biometric data. However, its use needs to be restricted.

**What you need Aadhaar for:**

- To pay taxes to the government
- To avail of the government's DBT schemes, such as those for cooking-gas cylinders and ration. However, no one can be denied these benefits for lack of Aadhaar or if authentication fails. In such instances, people must be able to use alternate identity proofs to claim benefits.

**What you do not need Aadhaar for:**

- Getting a SIM card for your mobile phone
- Opening a bank account and availing banking services
- Enrolling for all-India exams

Children can be enrolled with the consent of their parents or guardians, but they have the option to withdraw once they become adults. No child can be denied any benefit for not having Aadhaar. School admissions, for example, do not need Aadhaar.

UIDAI cannot store Aadhaar authentication data for more than six months.

Individuals and private companies cannot collect a person's Aadhaar data to verify their identity without consent.

No one can disclose Aadhaar information, even to the government, except by order of a court. If this happens, individuals should be able to lodge a complaint with authorities other than the UIDAI.

### Big Boss Is Watching

While the Aadhaar case generated considerable discussion around mass surveillance using technology, such surveillance has existed in India since the 1970s. Phone tapping—listening to and recording telephone conversations between people without their knowledge—was the earliest example of this practice. However, it was a deadly terrorist attack in Mumbai in 2008 that prompted the government to invest heavily in mass surveillance to strengthen India's internal security.

Even though governments have claimed that surveillance is necessary to monitor threats against national security, some people are uncomfortable because surveillance technology can also be used to gain unauthorized access to the personal data of users.

One of the most recent cases of illegal surveillance surfaced in 2021, when reports revealed that Pegasus—spyware developed by an Israeli company—had been used by the Indian government to secretly access phone calls, messages and emails of journalists, activists and political leaders critical of its rule. Investigations found malware in five out of twenty-nine phones checked but could not confirm if it was Pegasus.

## Making Laws

As the use of technology increased, governments in India passed laws to protect digital rights—the rights people enjoy when using technology such as the Internet. The first of these was the Information Technology (IT) Act, which was passed in 2000 to control cybercrime and make the Internet safer for people to use (*also see page 147*). Since then, the government has not only made changes to this Act but has also introduced newer laws, such as the Digital Personal Data Protection Act of 2023, to protect people's data and privacy online. Currently, the government is working on a comprehensive Digital India Act to ensure online safety, trust and accountability as well as an open Internet, and to regulate new-age technologies like artificial intelligence. As the use of technology evolves, the laws governing it are also going to change.

Sometimes, though, governments have been criticized for acting in ways that appear to compromise people's digital rights. For instance, on 12 September 2012, following protests in Kashmir against a movie that had hurt people's religious sentiments, the government imposed the first Internet shutdown in India. Although it only lasted for a few hours, it got the ball rolling. Since then, India has come to lead the world in imposing Internet shutdowns.

On their part, governments have claimed that Internet shutdowns are imposed for security reasons—turning off the Internet in areas affected by unrest stops people from circulating false information and other messages that can aggravate the situation. However, at a time when the Internet has become a way of life for many people, such shutdowns have caused much inconvenience and resentment.

**>800**

Number of Internet shutdowns in India between 2012 and 2024

During an eighteen-month Internet shutdown in Kashmir between 2019 and 2021—one of the longest in the world—petitions flooded the Supreme Court asking it to end the shutdown.

On 10 January 2020, the court ruled that access to the Internet was a part of the fundamental right to freedom of speech and expression granted to all Indians by the constitution, and an indefinite suspension of Internet services would be illegal—except in matters involving national security. Since the government was claiming national security concerns, instead of lifting the shutdown, the court urged it to reconsider its decision.

*'I once read on the Internet that speaking aloud while looking into a mirror can help to overcome a stammer, and that's what I began to do,' says Apar Gupta, recalling how access to the Internet during his school days helped him overcome a crippling stammer and discover a penchant for debating. The skill went on to play a significant role in his decision to be a lawyer and, as fate would have it, Apar ended up finding his calling in defending digital rights–the right to privacy in an ever-connected world–ensuring that Internet access was not governed by the business interests of Internet service providers and rallying against Internet shutdowns.*

*The cases, however, are not easy. Although Apar tries to remain detached from outcomes, this is not always possible. Internet shutdowns, for example, have been deeply disturbing. 'Every time the Internet is disrupted, one young person somewhere loses the means to read advice on what might be troubling them privately, address their insecurities and develop the full potential of their personality.' It is this overarching belief in the transformational power of the Internet that drives his work.*

## Citizens Take Action

Over the past few years, many citizens, civil society groups and non-governmental organizations have stepped forward to raise awareness about digital rights, question the fairness of digital laws, and take the government to court for flouting digital rights. Such activism has played a vital role in protecting these rights.

Among the most memorable examples of digital rights activism in India was against Section 66A of the Information Technology Act, which made it a crime to use social media, email or other messaging apps to send messages that were 'offensive' or caused 'annoyance, inconvenience, danger, obstruction, insult, injury, criminal intimidation, enmity, hatred or ill will'. However, the act offered no clarity on what could be considered 'offensive', 'annoying', etc., and the news regularly reported on how this was being misused to arrest people on seemingly trivial grounds.

In November 2012, college student Shaheen Dhada put up a post on Facebook criticizing the city-wide shutdown in Mumbai following the death of the politician Bal Thackeray. Her friend Renu Srinivasan liked the post and commented on it. Shortly afterwards, both girls were arrested by Mumbai police for flouting Section 66A! Like many people around the country, twenty-one-year-old Shreya Singhal was outraged by this: 'Facebook was very big in India at that time. I was on it. My friends were on it. What the arrests meant was that any of us could have ended up like Shaheen and Renu if we put up posts criticizing what the government was doing.'

In 2012, Shreya filed a petition against Section 66A in the Supreme Court. The case came up for hearing in 2014, and by March 2015, the judges had reached a verdict—Section 66A was invalid and had to be scrapped. The court noted how the lack of clarity in the law had meant that it had ended up curtailing 'a very large amount of protected and innocent speech'. This was a striking victory against a law that had long been used to harass people for speaking freely online.

From voting to governance, the role of modern technology has grown significantly in Indian democracy. But a democracy is a government of the people, by the people and for the people. So, any technology promoted by the government must have the interests of the people at its heart. If there are doubts over this, governments need to work with citizens to resolve them. Besides, as digital rights activism and victories, such as the one against Section 66A, have shown, in a democracy, citizens also have the power to influence how a government uses technology.

# 9

# Education, Health and Technology

Illiteracy and disease were among the most pressing problems facing newly independent India. More than 80 per cent of its population could neither read nor write and average life expectancy was just around thirty-six years. The leaders of independent India were eager to empower its people with education and healthcare. Could modern technology play a role in this? Many believed it could.

## Teaching with Tech

In a largely rural country where the majority could not read or write, radio and television offered a way of spreading education through informative programmes. However, the reach of such programmes was limited because India lacked the technology for long-distance broadcasts. This technology came to India in the 1960s, through its newborn space programme.

Founded in 1962, the Indian National Committee for Space Research (now known as the Indian Space Research Organisation or ISRO) wanted to utilize space technology to benefit the ordinary people of the country. One of its earliest endeavours was the Satellite Instructional Television Experiment (SITE)—using long-distance satellite transmission to expand the coverage of television broadcasts and spread the benefits of educational programmes.

Back in the day, India did not have a satellite of its own. So, ISRO struck a deal with the National Aeronautics and Space Administration (NASA) in the US to use its Applications Technology Satellite (ATS-6)—the largest, most powerful communications satellite of that time. In effect, the satellite would work like a TV tower situated more than

TV sets installed under SITE were fitted with simple chicken-mesh dish antennae to catch the satellite signal.

35,000 kilometres away in space from where it could beam programmes virtually anywhere in India.

The programmes were prepared in various Indian languages by the Centre for Education Technology that was founded in 1973. They were recorded at SITE studios in New Delhi, Cuttack and Bombay and delivered to Earth stations in Delhi and Ahmedabad. These Earth stations would uplink the programmes to NASA's satellite, which would transmit them to television sets that had been installed in thousands of villages across Andhra Pradesh, Karnataka, Bihar, Orissa (now Odisha), Madhya Pradesh and Rajasthan.

*Krishi Darshan* ('agriculture vision' in Hindi) was the first programme to air on Doordarshan, India's National Television Network.

Lakhs of viewers who had never seen television or cinema before were hooked to the broadcast—1.5 hours in the morning and 2.5 hours in the evening. Many of them were farmers who reported that agricultural programmes helped them understand new farming practices, including using the right kind and quantity of fertilizers in their fields.

Howard Galloway, a NASA representative who covered the experiment from India, wrote in one of his reports:

> 'Without exception, in all of the villages that we visited, the villagers sat quietly on the ground, on walls, on roofs, in trees, etc., with no talking and with an intense concentration on the screen. This

> behaviour was not exhibited for my benefit. I know this because until my photoflash went off, the folk were not aware of my presence.'

The experiment ran from August 1975 to July 1976. Despite several challenges, including irregular electricity supply and some faulty TV sets, SITE proved that technology could be used to teach people. It also introduced social change in villages by providing an avenue where people could gather to watch programmes on a common TV set, learn and enjoy themselves irrespective of social differences, such as gender and caste.

Even though NASA had to take back its satellite at the end of the year, the success of SITE prompted the government to fund the development of the Indian National Satellite (INSAT), one of the largest communication satellite systems in the Asia-Pacific. It was ready by the early 1980s and was used to continue broadcasting educational programmes, among other things.

In 1986, a decade after SITE, the government passed an education policy that actively encouraged the use of modern technology to spread the benefits of education. The National Literacy Mission (NLM) launched under this policy regarded the eradication of illiteracy as not just a social but also a technological undertaking. Apart from the use of radio and television broadcasts for learning, the policy encouraged the development of cheap and sturdy electronic teaching devices, and the enhancement of the learning environment through technologies, such as solar lamps, which could improve illumination in areas without electricity. However, the NLM's greatest inspiration came from a group of science writers and activists who had embarked on an ambitious mission to bring total literacy to the state of Kerala.

The Kerala Shastra Sahitya Parishad (KSSP) was founded in 1962 to popularize science education in the state. Total literacy had been one of its main objectives since the 1970s. During its annual meeting in 1987, the organization declared that it would take up an extensive programme to bring total literacy to the state within five years. Even though Kerala had fared better than most other Indian states in education, achieving total literacy was still some way off. But the road ahead wasn't easy, and the KSSP struggled. That's when the NLM, searching for a way to ignite India's motivation to learn, reached out to the KSSP and persuaded it to persist with the total literacy project in Kerala. On 26 January 1989, the KSSP launched the Ernakulam District Total Literacy Programme (EDTLP), which became a stunning success. Within a year, 1.75 lakh people in Ernakulam learnt to read and write for the very first time.

Literacy movement in Kerala

One of the key reasons behind EDTLP's success was a campaign that used folk songs, folk arts and street dramas to help unlettered people understand why illiteracy was a barrier in their lives, making them vulnerable to poverty and exploitation. By focusing on the needs of learners and using attractive ways to convey how education could improve their lives, the campaign captured the pulse of the people. It also motivated the literate population to join the programme and dispel illiteracy from their families and communities. Apart from holding processions and literacy foot marches, the campaign used radio and television programmes, pamphlets and other such means to disseminate its messages.

This idea was eventually scaled up nationwide by the National Council for Science and Technology Communication and came to be called the Bharat Gyan Vigyan Jatha. Thousands of writers, artists, actors and students from different states came together to create a compelling procession that went around the country between October and November 1990, inspiring more Indians to take up education.

A lot of people in India did not end up with an education because they were too old, underqualified or there was no educational institution near their homes. To overcome such hurdles, Delhi University introduced distance education in 1962. Soon afterwards, distance education courses spread to universities in other states. In 1985 the government established the Indira Gandhi National Open University (IGNOU), and in 1989, it also established the National Open School (now called the National Institute of Open Schooling or NIOS). Not bound to physical classrooms, such education was open to everyone, regardless of age, qualification or location. While the postal network was used to send typed or photocopied study materials to students, the spread of technology came to play a vital role in increasing the reach of distance education and bridging the gap between teachers and students.

The development of INSAT enhanced radio and television broadcasts used for distance education. By 2000, IGNOU had launched India's first dedicated educational TV channel, Gyan Darshan, which provided twenty-four-hour educational content to viewers. The very next year, it began Gyan Vani, an educational radio network operating through ten stations in various parts of the country. In 2004, India launched EDUSAT—the first satellite dedicated exclusively to delivering educational content. Even though satellite-supported broadcasts widened the reach of distance education, it was the rapid spread of digital technology, particularly in the years since 2010, that truly revolutionized it. Internet-enabled smartphones not only made such courses and educational resources available at the click of a button to learners even in the remotest parts of the country but also made it easier for them to connect with teachers online.

* * *

Till the 1980s, the use of technology was largely restricted to institutes of technical education and research. However, in 1984, the government began the Computer Literacy and Studies in Schools programme, bringing children in more than 200 government schools face to face with microcomputers for the very first time.

This created quite a buzz in some quarters. Many people found much merit in computer-aided education. Among them was Sugata Mitra, who worked at the National Institute of Information Technology. Mitra had been researching the possibilities of learning through computers. Towards the end of the 1990s, he began the Hole-in-the-Wall experiment. Under this experiment, Internet-enabled personal computers were installed in various poor neighbourhoods of Delhi and left unattended to see how children engaged with them. According to Mitra, children without any knowledge of English or computing glued themselves to the machines and began experimenting with them. Within a few months, without any assistance from a teacher, the children had learned multiple new skills and shared them with their friends. Mitra reported similar results when he conducted the experiment in other states. This led him to conclude that computers could play a vital role in learning, especially in places where access to high-quality teaching was limited. But could computers really make up for the lack of good teaching? Investigations uncovered that in the absence of teachers, children using the Hole-in-the-Wall computers (where they had not been stolen, abandoned or vandalized) often ended up spending most of their time playing games. Moreover, older boys dominated the machines, leaving fewer opportunities for younger children.

Children glued themselves to the Hole-in-the-Wall computers

By the beginning of the new millennium, computers had entered lakhs of schools—but they had not entered classrooms. Instead, they were restricted to separate computer laboratories or rooms where they were accessed as an extracurricular activity or as part of an optional subject on computing offered by some schools. This began to change with the advent of the smart classroom in 2004. In these classrooms, the chalkboard gave way to a computerized projector that screened lessons on a digital or smart board. However, the technology was expensive, and most schools could not afford it. Many educationists also felt that it was driven more by technological considerations than by the actual needs of teachers. The content, for example, was often out of sync with what was being taught in classrooms. As tech providers played catch-up with the needs of educators, the popularity of education technology began to grow. From helping with school admissions to tutoring children in different subjects, education technology companies were soon offering a variety of services, but the device that led to an explosion in such offerings was the smartphone.

For crores of Indians, the smartphone was their first radio, television, camera, computer and telephone rolled into one nifty, portable gadget. By 2010, smartphones had become affordable for more Indians, and mobile connectivity had improved with the introduction of the 3G network. Shortly thereafter, the advent of 4G networks increased Internet speed even more. A few years later, the cost of accessing the Internet on smartphones dropped dramatically. These developments spurred an expansion in mobile-based learning apps. Yet, it was the COVID-19 pandemic that truly became a game changer for education technology as it confined crores of Indians to their homes and compelled education institutions to teach students online.

Many educators and students got a first-hand experience of how technology could be actively used to impart education during the pandemic years. Keeping pace with the changes, the government announced a new education policy in 2020 that expanded the use of education technology in India. Under this policy, it established the National Educational Technology Forum—a special body to engage with new technologies and advise the government on how these technologies could be used in education.

However, the pandemic also revealed the limitations of online education. Crores of children lost valuable years of learning because they did not have the means to study online. Many lacked access to devices such as computers and mobile phones, either because their families were too poor to afford such devices or because many family members were sharing one device and could not spare it all the time for online classes. Moreover, online classes required greater supervision at home and regular electricity supply, which many households could not manage. Without regular schooling, a large number of children belonging to poor families could not continue their studies because they got pulled into housework and helping their parents make a living.

There is no denying that access to technology has increased significantly in the years since Independence. The Annual Status of Education Report 2023 found that nearly 90 per cent of all youth have access to a smartphone at home and know how to use it. The growth in education technology only mirrors this wider transformation, but the impact of this growth on actual learning remains uncertain. While India has created many technological resources for education, most experts agree that it needs to do more to ensure that all educators and learners can use these resources effectively.

## Treating with Tech

Poor public health had been a problem in India long before Independence. Diseases such as smallpox, tuberculosis, malaria and cholera claimed lakhs of lives every year. So, it wasn't surprising that the earliest use of modern technology in healthcare was the development of medicines and vaccines to combat these diseases.

In 1946, a year before Independence, India started exploring the possibility of manufacturing antibiotics such as penicillin, which could treat a range of common bacterial infections. By 1949, it was ready to set up a factory. However, it lacked the necessary technology to do this and needed foreign assistance. Various foreign companies came forward, but the best offer that India received was from the American company Merck, which was willing to bring in its technology to help set up a penicillin factory in return for a steep fee. The other companies were only willing to bottle imported penicillin in India.

At the time, such deals were common. In a country which lacked technically skilled workers, as well as basic infrastructure such as roads and electricity, many industrialists favoured importing foreign technology instead of struggling to build it locally. Although the government tended to mistrust foreign companies, it realized the pressing need for such collaborations. However, just as it was mulling over Merck's offer, the World Health Organization (WHO) and the United Nations International Children's Emergency Fund (UNICEF) came forward with a proposal to help India set up the factory and also train Indian scientists, engineers and technicians on how to run it. In return, they wanted India to share its research and discoveries with a network of similar centres the UN was setting up in other developing countries.

Prime Minister Jawaharlal Nehru decided to go ahead with the global bodies, and by 1954, India was home to Hindustan Antibiotics—the first factory in the developing world to manufacture critical medicines. Various research laboratories, such as the Regional Research Laboratory in Hyderabad (now called the Indian Institute of Chemical Technology), were also set up in the 1950s to develop the technology necessary for producing medicines locally. This, however, was a slow process, and until 1970, most medicines sold in India were being produced by big brands in Europe and the US. The technology used to make these medicines was protected by law, so Indian companies could not use it easily.

In 1970, the government passed a landmark law that radically transformed India's ability to manufacture all kinds of medicines on its own. Under this law, Indian companies were allowed to produce the medicines, so long as they did not copy the process used by the foreign brands. This, though, was easier said than done. Companies needed to study the foreign medicines carefully, accurately guess the ingredients and methods used and then produce the same medicine, with the same effect, using a slightly different manufacturing process. Yet, Indian research laboratories and medicine makers accomplished this reverse engineering of foreign medicines with great success. Over the next few decades, the number of Indian companies making such generic (non-branded) medicines multiplied, while many foreign medicine makers left the country. Local manufacturing meant that not only were the medicines cheaper, but they were also more easily available. The technological expertise and skills acquired by Indian medicine makers in the years since 1970 have turned India into the world's pharmacy. Today, low-cost medicines produced in India not only help fight against diseases within the country but also across the world.

* * *

Frequent outbreaks of diseases and the rising death toll had prompted the British government to start manufacturing and administering vaccines in India during the nineteenth century. Various research laboratories were set up across the country. Among these was the Plague Research Laboratory established in Bombay (now Mumbai) in 1899, where the Russia-born scientist Waldemar Mordecai Haffkine created the world's earliest vaccines for plague and cholera. However, such facilities could not produce enough vaccines to meet the immense burden of diseases in newly independent India. Moreover, the country lacked the infrastructure and trained workforce needed to carry out mass vaccination programmes.

This situation changed by the 1970s as the number of vaccine manufacturing units increased, improving India's vaccine-making capabilities. Much like the medicine manufacturers, these units used reverse engineering to produce low-cost versions of various foreign vaccines in India. Meanwhile, the government began mass vaccination (immunization) programmes, which proved highly successful in controlling diseases such as smallpox and polio. Greater availability of trained workers and improvements in transportation and cold storage facilities were hugely beneficial in this pursuit.

In 1977, India was declared smallpox-free, and in 2014, it was certified polio-free. Encouraged by its success in eradicating smallpox, the government began the Expanded Programme of Immunization in 1978 for diphtheria, pertussis, tetanus, polio, tuberculosis and typhoid. This programme was renamed the Universal Immunization Programme (UIP) in 1985 and expanded beyond urban areas. Today, more than two crore newborns and nearly three crore pregnant women in India are immunized under the UIP every year. India-made vaccines are also used to immunize more than half the children born worldwide against life-threatening diseases.

Unlike its remarkable success with medicines and vaccines, India made slow progress in manufacturing medical devices. Lacking the expertise and industrial infrastructure to produce high-tech devices like CT scanners and MRI machines, it came to depend heavily on imports and continues to buy such machines from countries like the US, Germany, Japan and Singapore. However, the need for affordable medical technology in a country struggling with poverty has encouraged various low-cost innovations. The Jaipur foot, an artificial low-cost limb developed in the city of Jaipur in 1968, for instance, has helped countless amputees walk again, while the Chitra heart valve, an indigenously developed mechanical heart valve, has saved many people suffering from heart damage since 1990.

Jaipur foot

Most of all, India has struggled to provide adequate, accessible and affordable healthcare facilities to its people.

A few years before Independence, the British government had set up a Health Survey and Development Committee headed by an official named Joseph Bhore. The purpose of the committee was to assess health conditions prevailing in British India and make recommendations for future development. Among the committee's key recommendations was establishing a robust and affordable healthcare delivery system, beginning with primary healthcare units at the village level that would bring essential medical care to the doorstep of most Indians. These units would need to be supported by bigger and more advanced facilities serving a larger population. However, creating such infrastructure required substantial government funding, which was hard to obtain. The dearth of such infrastructure has meant that India's technological progress in healthcare has often failed to touch the lives of ordinary Indians. An early example of this could be seen in India's efforts to control malaria.

At the time of Independence, nearly eight lakh people died of malaria every year in India. Technology in the form of the pesticide dichloro-diphenyl-trichloroethane, commonly known as DDT, offered a formidable weapon against the malaria-causing mosquito. In a country with inadequate healthcare facilities, large-scale spraying of cheaply imported DDT seemed like a convenient, cost-effective solution to eradicate malaria, and the government was quick to adopt it. In 1953, under the National Malaria Control Programme, squads armed with DDT were dispatched to places with the highest number of malaria cases in the country. The programme was such a resounding success that by 1958, the government had scaled it nationwide, renaming it the National Malaria Eradication Programme. Powered by DDT, India appeared to be winning the battle against malaria. But these gains were short-lived. By the late 1960s, the disease had returned with a vengeance, forcing the government to take emergency measures. What had gone wrong?

According to some experts, the mosquitoes had become resistant to DDT, but this wasn't the only reason. Spraying DDT was not enough to control malaria. The malaria control teams also needed to locate all infected individuals in an area and treat them with anti-malarial medicines. Unless all infected individuals were treated, the mosquitoes could easily transmit the disease from them to others. However, this required effective healthcare delivery systems as envisioned by the Bhore Committee. The lack of such systems meant that controlling diseases like malaria would continue to remain a challenge in most parts of India.

Spraying DDT for malaria control

In 1983, India framed its first National Health Policy. Struggling to fund adequate healthcare facilities for the country's growing population, the government proposed expanding the role of the private sector under this policy. This led to the birth of Apollo, India's first corporate hospital, in 1984 and a virtually unstoppable growth in private healthcare that soon surpassed government-funded public healthcare systems.

The well-heeled and widespread private sector became a hub for advances in medical technology. One of the major technological advancements introduced by India's private healthcare system was telemedicine—using telecommunications technology to deliver medical services in remote areas. This began in 2001 when ISRO linked the Apollo hospital in the city of Chennai with an Apollo rural hospital at Aragonda village in Andhra Pradesh. Between 2003 and 2004, ISRO improved the satellite-based communication infrastructure required for telemedicine. By 2005, the Ministry of Health and Family Welfare had set up a telemedicine task force, that paved the way for many projects using this technology. Growing connectivity through mobile phones and the Internet during the 2000s further expanded the reach of telemedicine.

Despite such advances, India continued to be plagued by insufficient healthcare. Many civil society groups felt that healthcare in India had come to depend too much on private hospitals and clinics, which appeared to be focusing on treatment using the latest medical technology while overlooking social factors, such as food, hygiene and people's willingness and ability to seek treatment.

To address these deficiencies, the government launched the National Rural Health Mission (NRHM) in 2005. One of the largest public health programmes since Independence, the NRHM hoped to fulfil India's longstanding ambition of taking accessible, affordable and quality healthcare to the doorstep of every person living in its villages. The biggest accomplishment of this mission was community participation in healthcare, in the form of Accredited Social Health Activists (ASHAs).

The ASHAs were women from local communities, with a minimum education up to the eighth standard, who were trained in basic health issues, such as the need for immunization, giving birth in medical institutions instead of homes and the importance of maintaining clean surroundings. Following the training, they were expected to create awareness around these issues within their communities and become a crucial link between the people and primary healthcare. The ASHAs were also equipped with medical kits to treat common ailments, such as tablets for fevers and Oral Rehydration Solution for diarrhoea, vomiting and heat strokes. Although they were not regular employees, they were offered incentives based on their performance.

More than eight lakh ASHAs were trained under the NRHM. Despite problems such as inadequate training and insufficient and delayed incentives, they played a vital role in improving rural healthcare, especially for women and children. More women began to give birth in medical institutions, and more children were vaccinated against preventable diseases. In 2015, the NRHM became part of the National Health Mission and was expanded to include underserved urban areas. Unfortunately, as it grew, the mission could not sustain community participation. Meanwhile, the emphasis on digitalization expanded. In 2017, the government announced a national health policy that made a major push to enhance healthcare delivery using digital technology, such as telemedicine and electronic health records.

The COVID-19 pandemic, which began in 2020, laid bare the successes and failures of India's approach to healthcare since Independence. Lakhs of Indians were able to consult doctors online using telemedicine services. Technological advancements in researching and developing vaccines meant that Indian scientists were able to collaborate with international scientists to gather all the essential information on the disease within weeks and begin trials for Covaxin, a locally developed vaccine, by May 2020. From 16 January 2021, India began vaccinating people with Covaxin, as well as Covishield, another vaccine that had been developed in the UK but was being manufactured in India. By March 2022, India had vaccinated more than 80 per cent of its adult population—an extraordinary achievement in the world's most populated country. In addition to meeting the needs of its own people, India was also able to continue supplying medicines and vaccines to the rest of the world. These impressive records, however, stood in sharp contrast to the failures in its public health system.

Towards the end of April 2021, India became the first country in the world to report four lakh infections in a single day. A new variant of the COVID-19 virus was spreading rapidly across the country, including its rural districts, which had largely remained safe until then. It infected the respiratory system so severely that many patients needed artificial oxygen to breathe. But India did not possess enough oxygen cylinders, and these had to be urgently imported. Meanwhile, its overstretched healthcare system suffered a massive meltdown. People were running from pillar to post in search of hospital beds, doctors, nurses and oxygen cylinders. Private hospitals and clinics were charging astronomical prices for treatment. Many patients, especially in underserved rural areas, died because they ran out of breath before they could get any medical assistance. Between 1 May and 26 May, more than 80 lakh people were infected, and over a lakh died. Room for cremating the dead ran out.

Despite its remarkable technological achievements, India's record in healthcare was held up to question.

In 2016, the WHO had determined that countries needed at least one doctor for every 1,000 people to meet the minimum requirement for adequate healthcare. In 2022, Union Health Minister Mansukh Mandaviya declared that India had one doctor for every 834 people—better than the WHO's standard. Given the expansion in medical education, India has indeed been producing more doctors. But does this mean that everyone in the country has easy access to a good doctor? Not necessarily. Many doctors work in private hospitals and clinics in urban areas, which are not accessible or affordable for everyone.

Despite all its shortcomings, healthcare in India has made a significant improvement in life expectancy. The greater availability of medicines, vaccines and other treatment options has meant that Indians are living much longer than they did at the time of Independence. But in the world's most populated country, this also means that the need for healthcare facilities is far greater. While technological advancements have strengthened healthcare, they cannot be expected to replace the need for accessible, affordable and skilled doctors, nurses, healthcare workers and medical institutions.

## Last Words

From landing a spacecraft on Mars in its very first attempt to building a thriving IT industry, in the years since Independence,

India's technological progress has become the stuff of legends. Yet, the success of technological development has been limited in the fields of education and healthcare. This is because technology does not hold the key to better education and healthcare. Humans do. They can be empowered by it but not replaced. So even as the government pushes the use of technology in education and healthcare, it must not lose sight of the humans—the teachers, doctors, nurses, workers—who fulfil these crucial social needs.

*Nidesh Soni had been working with the Eklavya Foundation at Shahpur, in Madhya Pradesh's Betul district, for more than a decade when the COVID-19 pandemic struck havoc. Talking about Eklavya's role during the pandemic, Nidesh says, 'Most of our work was in education. We used to work with children to develop literacy and numeracy, but during the pandemic we decided to work on health along with education.'*

*By May 2021, the Eklavya team, along with a few others, had started a telemedicine network with Indian and foreign doctors who were offering free online consultations to the people in Shahpur.*

*Recalling the experience, Nidesh says, 'Most of us had Internet-enabled smartphones, as did many people in Shahpur. We downloaded a video-calling app on the available smartphones and fixed consultation times. We also translated the conversation and the medical prescription for patients.' He further adds that many residents were astonished at the idea of getting medical advice on their phones. They could not believe it. Many mistrusted it initially. They thought it was too good to be true.*

*Nevertheless, the facility proved to be deeply transformative. One young woman afflicted with COVID-19, who had returned to Shahpur from the city and had almost given up all hope of surviving, made a miraculous recovery with advice and help from the telemedicine network. Supplies, such as an oxygen concentrator and monitor, were arranged for her by the doctors and the volunteers.*

*Along the way, the volunteers learnt more about conducting basic health checks for fever, blood sugar and blood pressure. They also learnt about mental health problems. Regular medical consultations also uncovered some surprising health problems plaguing the town. Many people suffered from serious skin diseases, high blood pressure and diabetes because they worked outdoors without any precautions and ate food that lacked the necessary nutrition.*

*'So many people had been enduring so much pain for years because of fungal infections that went undiscovered and untreated. Doctors in the telemedicine network identified these, bringing enormous relief,' says Nidesh.*

*By the time the pandemic subsided in 2022, thousands of people in Shahpur and surrounding areas had benefitted from the telemedicine network. Their medical records had been saved in a database for future consultations, and healthcare had become part of the team's work.*

*Nidesh feels that education takes years to show its benefits, but healthcare shows results immediately. 'Good healthcare improves people's lives almost instantly. People began to look at us and our work very differently after we began to help them with medical care.'*

*Although the local people now address the volunteers as Doctor Bhaiya, Nidesh is deeply grateful to the actual doctors who volunteered their time. 'None of this would have worked if they had not agreed to help.'*

# 10

# Environment and Technology

Life in newly independent India was very different from what it is today. Most people lived in villages surrounded by farmland, rivers and mountains. There were very few roads and they were mostly bad, so people walked a lot and seldom travelled far. When they did, they used bullock carts, bicycles or the railway—cars were largely unheard of. Even electricity was virtually unknown—oil lamps were used for lighting and pankhas (hand fans) for cooling. Modern technology was visibly missing in ordinary Indian life.

Slowly, however, things began to change. Towering dams came up on large rivers, diverting water for farms and households and generating hydroelectricity. Factories began to produce everything from gleaming steel to big machines. Roads were paved and motor vehicles began to ply on them, making it easier for people to travel. Electricity spread around the country, lighting up homes. Excited by these 'great engineering works', Prime Minister Jawaharlal wrote: 'They are visible symbols of building up the new India and of providing life and sustenance to our people.'

Technology powered development, bringing many comforts that we often take for granted today. But it came at a cost—the conquest of nature.

## Developmental Distress

The 1970s and 1980s brought a wave of protests against this assault on nature. Some of the most prominent protests emerged in the Himalayan villages of Uttarakhand (then part of Uttar Pradesh). Relentless deforestation, damming, mining and road building in the steep and unstable Himalayas had led to deadly floods, landslides, slope failures and other environmental catastrophes that put people's lives and livelihood in danger. Agitated by this, the people of Uttarakhand hugged their trees to stop industries from cutting them down, protested against the construction of the Tehri Dam and gave up on the ways of the Green Revolution, returning to traditional seeds and old ways of farming (*also see page 82*).

Elsewhere, too, ordinary Indians were demonstrating against reckless development. At Silent Valley in Kerala, people opposed a dam that would drown a rainforest and endanger the natural habitat of the lion-tailed macaque. Along the river Narmada, they rallied against the Sardar Sarovar Dam that would displace more than two lakh people. Some of these movements succeeded in halting development projects; others did not. However, all of them helped turn India's attention towards the environmental cost of development.

Environmental issues started appearing more regularly in the news, and more people began talking about them. This put pressure on the government, often prompting it to act against environmental violations. The greatest turning point came one night in December 1984 when a technical failure at the Union Carbide pesticide factory in Bhopal led to a poisonous gas leak that killed thousands of people. Investigations revealed that the accident was a result of extreme industrial negligence. Workers had complained about faulty equipment and poor operation and maintenance previously. However, the factory was incurring losses and the corporation wanted to reduce its operating costs. So, it did nothing to address the complaints and ensure safety.

## Industrial Pollution

Factories, like the one in Bhopal, were a major cause of environmental degradation in independent India. They extracted raw materials such as water and minerals from the environment and released waste that polluted land, water bodies and the air. Yet, in its quest for rapid industrialization, India largely overlooked these dangers.

The Bhopal gas tragedy shocked the country and compelled it to act against unsafe industrialization. A year after the disaster, the government established a separate Ministry of Environment and Forests (now called the Ministry of Environment, Forests and Climate Change or MoEFCC) to oversee all environmental policies and programmes. In 1986, it passed the historic Environmental Protection Act to control industrial pollution, punish polluters and safeguard India's natural resources. By 1994, it had become necessary for industries to submit a detailed report on the environmental impact of any new project, such as a factory or mine, to the government. Based on this Environmental Impact Assessment report, the government would evaluate the project and either permit or reject it.

The strengthening of environmental laws during the 1980s and 1990s encouraged many individuals and non-governmental organizations to take environmental issues to court. One of the first such cases before the Supreme Court was related to limestone mining in Uttarakhand's Doon

Valley. Citizen groups in the valley wanted the mining to stop. Limestone, they said, played a vital role in absorbing rainwater, which prevented deadly floods during the monsoon and ensured water supply for the region's rivers during the dry season. Mining companies, on the other hand, asserted that limestone was an important raw material for several industries that manufactured things people needed, and offered employment to many. The court had to weigh both arguments and decide whether conserving limestone was indeed better than mining it.

By 1988, the court had arrived at a decision—more than 100 limestone mines in the Doon Valley were ordered to close down. Even though limestone was an important industrial raw material, the court observed that mining it in an ecologically sensitive region like Uttarakhand was dangerous and threatened the natural environment, as well as the lives of local people.

## E-Waste

Newly independent India was largely a stranger to electronic devices. These were usually imported from other countries and cost a small fortune. During the 1980s, the government began to encourage electronics in a big way. It wanted the crucial electronics industry to grow, and this would only be possible if more Indians used electronic devices in their everyday life.

In 1991, India's economy changed in a big way and business boomed (*also see pages 15–16*). Growing prosperity revealed itself in the things Indians were buying and throwing away. One of the greatest environmental crises caused by modern technology showed up in India's garbage, which slowly started overflowing with discarded electronics.

## E-Waste in India

India has been casting away such astonishing amounts of e-waste that in 2024, it became the third-largest e-waste producer in the world, after the US and China.

**>17,00,000 MT (metric tonnes)**

of e-waste is generated in India every year

**>1,000**

different substances make up e-waste, many of which are hazardous for humans and the environment

## What's in your e-waste?

**50%**

ferrous (iron and steel)

**21%**

plastics

**13%**

non-ferrous materials

**>80%**

e-waste is personal devices

**16%**

others (glass, wood, concrete, ceramics, rubber, etc.)

Source: Research Unit (LARRDIS) Rajya Sabha Secretariat, 'E-Waste in India,' June 2011; Dinesh Raj Bandela, 'E-Waste Day: 82% of India's E-Waste is Personal Devices,' *Down to Earth*, 13 October 2018; and Kiran Pandey, 'India's E-Waste Surges by 73% in 5 Years,' *Down to Earth*, 17 December 2024.

Examine any electronic device around you. It will most likely have a body made of plastic and glass. If you look within, you will find an intricate circuit made up of several different components. Tonnes of metals, such as aluminium, copper, gold and silver, are mined to make these components. The mines scar the landscape and discharge toxic waste that pollutes surrounding areas. Next come the factories where these metals are transformed into necessary components, assembled into finished devices, packaged and sent out for selling. These factories add to the environmental cost of electronics. The problem, however, is significantly compounded by electronic waste (e-waste)—electronics that people cast off after using.

During the 2000s, e-waste was categorized under hazardous wastes. However, alarm bells went off in April 2010, when unsuspecting workers dismantling electronic equipment at a scrap market in Delhi suffered serious radiation injuries, which killed one of them. A year later, the MoEFCC passed the E-waste (Management and Handling) Rules, making India the only country in South Asia to have a law dedicated to this variety of waste.

The law classified e-waste into different categories such as household appliances, medical equipment and office electronics, and held electronic manufacturers responsible for managing it. Having such a law has encouraged the growth of e-waste recycling in India—in 2024, India had more than 400 authorized recyclers compared to just twenty-three in 2010. Unfortunately, a majority of this waste is collected and recycled in ways that pose grave danger to people and the environment.

Most e-waste is collected by *kabadiwallas* or scrap dealers and taken to scrap markets like the ones at Seelampur in Delhi or Dharavi in Mumbai.

In these scrap markets, workers in small, informal recycling establishments take e-waste apart using hammers and pliers. They mainly extract precious metals such as gold and copper, which fetch the highest value when sold for further recycling.

The workers work without any protective gear and engage in harmful activities such as burning wires and dipping circuit boards in acid. Since the establishments are unauthorized, the government has no formal record of their existence. This makes it easy for them to violate laws and ignore safety.

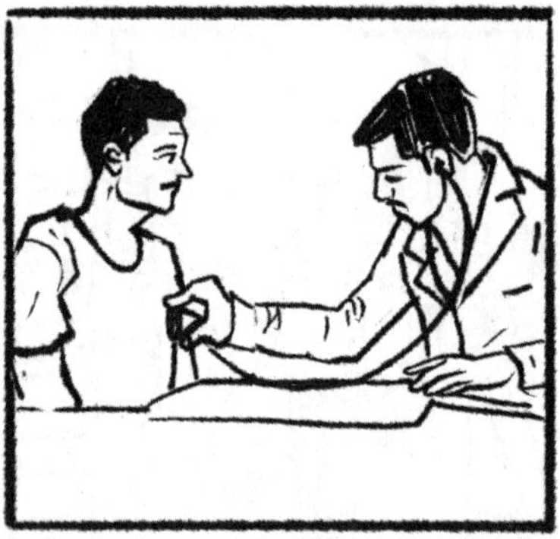

Health problems, particularly breathing difficulties and skin infections are common among waste workers. Many children are also engaged in this work, especially in collecting discarded parts.

Whatever remains at the end of this recycling exercise usually ends up in landfills or rivers, severely polluting these sites.

Over time, many scrap markets have become highly specialized in dealing with particular kinds of e-waste. About half the circuit boards used in electronic appliances in India are believed to end up in the city of Moradabad in Uttar Pradesh for recycling.

Despite the dangers posed by it, recycling of e-waste is a growing industry. Extracting metals this way is usually more energy-efficient and cost-effective than mining them. That's why electronics manufacturers have a very good reason to promote e-waste recycling. However, instead of backing various technologies that have been invented for recycling discarded electronics, many companies continue to support informal recycling done by hand because it costs much less.

Organizing the collection and recycling of e-waste into an authorized business is an important step in controlling the hazards posed by informal recycling. It encourages recyclers to follow the law and improve their processes, reducing the negative impact on the health of waste workers and the natural environment. Moreover, it puts the entire operation on record, making it easier to track what happens to electronics once they are discarded.

Having recognized this, many non-governmental organizations and private companies are working towards transforming e-waste recycling into an organized, sustainable and profitable business. On its part, the government has been updating laws and policies to keep pace with the growing amount and varieties of e-waste. For instance, in 2022, it revised the E-waste (Management and Handling) Rules to encourage companies to keep a digital record of e-waste management and restrict the use of highly toxic substances, like mercury, lead and cadmium in manufacturing electrical and electronic equipment. However, any initiative to improve e-waste recycling must take care of the needs of the vast number of informal workers and encourage them to change.

Electronics manufacturers also need to be encouraged to control e-waste. After all, the more gadgets they sell, the more money they make—even if many of these gadgets end up as waste. While using recycled metals is one way to make their business sustainable, there are many other ways too.

To promote newer devices, many manufacturers deliberately make their old devices obsolete. For example, they stop producing spare parts necessary to repair and maintain old devices or they add upgrades that end up slowing down the performance of older models. Is it possible to stop them from doing this and encourage them to manufacture more long-lasting devices? Laws in many countries require electronics manufacturers to take back old devices from consumers and recycle them sustainably. However, most manufacturers either do not follow through or do not publicize this practice. Ultimately, it is consumers of electronics who have a vital responsibility in controlling e-waste.

### What Can You Do to Control E-Waste?

- The longer you use your gadgets, the more money you will save and the less you will contribute to e-waste—don't get waylaid by fancy advertisements about the latest gizmos!
- If a gadget develops a fault, opting for repair is more eco-friendly than discarding it.
- Always check on repair and maintenance policies when you purchase a new electronic device—this will go a long way in encouraging electronics manufacturers to improve these services. In 2022, the Department of Consumer Affairs launched the Right to Repair portal, where users can access repair information for products from a variety of brands.

- If you have no option but to discard, avoid handing over your e-waste to an informal waste collector. Instead, search for registered collection organizations in your city. Some NGOs you can approach for this are Group TenPlus, Karo Sambhav, Swach and Toxic Links.
- Reach out to the electronic manufacturer and check if they take back old devices—most of them should.

## Toxic Trade

Believe it or not, many countries around the world have also been exporting and importing e-waste since the 1980s! Wondering why they did this? It made business sense.

Recycling ever-growing heaps of e-waste was far more expensive in wealthy countries, and manufacturers could not ignore strictly enforced environmental laws. So, shipping the waste to poorer countries where recycling was cheaper and laws were either non-existent or loosely enforced was convenient and cost-effective. For the poorer countries, recycling this waste became a source of revenue, valuable metals and jobs. However, this practice of dumping hazardous waste into poorer countries was widely criticized.

In 1988, Koko, a tiny port town in Nigeria, hit international headlines when highly toxic waste dumped there by ships from Italy leaked into the soil and groundwater, making local residents seriously ill. An international operation was carried out to clear the waste and send it back to Italy, where it was disposed of under the much stricter Italian laws. The very next year, the UN adopted the Basel Convention on the Control of Transboundary Movements of Hazardous Wastes and Their Disposal. This was the first major global effort to combat this toxic trade. The agreement made it necessary for countries to give written consent before waste was imported into their territory. Meanwhile, exporters needed to ensure that the waste would be handled in an environmentally safe way by the importer.

India, which joined the Basel Convention in 1992, was among the first few countries to urge for a ban on the export of hazardous waste. Ironically, it has since become one of the world's largest importers of e-waste. In 2022, for example, India imported over 2,40,000 metric tonnes of e-waste and scrap.

## Green Technology?

Even though modern technology has led to serious environmental problems, technological progress has also helped India in battling these challenges.

Air pollution is one of the most pressing environmental issues in India. The country has a majority of the world's most polluted cities, including its capital, New Delhi. Polluted air is filled with particulate matter—solid particles and liquid droplets several times smaller than a strand of human hair.

When these particles enter the body, they can pose serious health risks. Lakhs of people die because of air pollution in India every year.

Burning fossil fuels, such as coal and oil, to generate electricity is one of the leading causes of air pollution. Over the past few decades, India has been ambitiously promoting the use of renewable energy to replace fossil fuels.

## How Do Fossil Fuels Hurt the Environment?

Fossil fuels, such as coal and natural gas, originate from the remains of prehistoric plants and animals buried under the earth for millions of years. When burned, these fuels release carbon and hydrogen in the form of various gases and smoke. This not only pollutes the air but also traps heat, contributing to global warming.

Moreover, fossil fuels are non-renewable—which means they will not last forever—and given the rate at which they are being used, they are likely to disappear sooner than later. Despite this, the quest to find alternative sources of energy only took root in the 1970s, when problems in the Middle East, a leading supplier of fossil fuels, paused global supplies and plunged many countries into an energy crisis. This led to the rise of renewable energy drawn from sources such as wind and sunlight that are replenished much faster than they are consumed.

Wind was the first major source of renewable energy used for generating electricity in India. The first wind farms were set up in the 1980s at Ratnagiri in Maharashtra, Okha in Gujarat and Tuticorin in Tamil Nadu—all coastal areas with high wind speeds. When the initial experiment succeeded, more wind farms came up in other windy areas of the country. Today, India has hundreds of wind farms where fan-like blades fixed on tall poles, rip through windy air, harvesting its energy to generate electricity.

India receives around 250 to 300 days of sunshine in a year. Much like the wind, sunlight contains vast amounts of energy, and India has long been experimenting with its uses. One of the first indigenous technologies to come out of Indian research laboratories was the solar cooker. On 21 March 1952, newspapers reported that Prime Minister Jawaharlal Nehru had eaten 'sun-cooked' vegetables from a solar cooker installed in his home! In a largely rural country, it was expected that the cooker would reduce the dependence on cow dung as a cooking fuel and make more of it available as manure for farming. But the device failed to take off. Priced at fifty rupees, it was prohibitively expensive for rural India at the time. The cooker's body collected dust and over time, lost its shine, reducing its ability to utilize sunlight. Moreover, the invention did not bear in mind the realities of rural life—farmers set out for work close to sunrise when the cooker could not be used. Despite this, India did not give up its quest to harvest solar energy and experimented with other solar-powered devices, such as water heaters and lamps.

During the 1990s, Indian scientists began exploring the use of solar cells that converted solar energy directly into electricity. However, the technology was advanced and costly, and it needed extensive government support.

Solar or photovoltaic (PV) cells are made up of semiconductor materials like silicon that absorb sunlight and eventually dislodge it as electricity. Several cells are grouped together to form one solar panel.

Supplying electricity to different parts of India had proved to be a challenge. The electric grid had not been able to reach everywhere. What if villages, especially in remote areas, were able to harness electricity directly from the sun instead of relying on the grid? The government recognized the potential in this, and during the early 2000s, different villages were taken up for electrification using solar energy. In 2010, India announced the National Solar Mission to promote solar power. As solar power spread across the country, the technology improved and costs reduced.

## Meet India's Solar Mamas!

Can ordinary village women, most of them mothers and grandmothers who never went to school, become mechanics and engineers? Yes!

This revolutionary idea has been Sanjit 'Bunker' Roy's life's work. In 1972, he established the Barefoot College in Tilonia, Rajasthan, to train uneducated local communities to meet their needs by adopting suitable technologies and skills. Women have been among its greatest beneficiaries.

When solar technology started gaining ground in India, the Barefoot College began to train village communities in it. Many of its trainees were uneducated women. Using inventive teaching practices, the college taught the women how to install, operate and maintain solar power systems in their villages and fabricate devices such as solar lamps.

By 2023, India had developed the capacity to generate 179 gigawatts of electricity using renewable energy, of which solar and wind made up sixty-seven gigawatts and forty-three gigawatts, respectively. Yet, actual electricity production from these sources remains low. One of the reasons behind this is unsteady supply. The sun only shines for a few hours a day, and its intensity varies. For example, it doesn't shine brightly on rainy days. Meanwhile, the wind may blow in a different direction or not at all. To overcome this shortcoming, India has been building its capacity to store large amounts of solar power so that it can be used even when the sun isn't shining. One of the most inventive ways it's doing this is by marrying solar energy with hydroelectricity.

Typically, dams release water from a great height on to turbines, which turn the power of the falling water into hydroelectricity. Raising the water, however, also requires electricity, and recently, India has started exploring solar power for doing this. Known as solar-driven pumped storage hydropower, this system involves two interconnected reservoirs—one higher than the other. During the day, solar power is used to pump water from the lower to the higher reservoir, which releases the water to produce electricity when demand peaks. This system works like a giant water battery that stores and uses renewable energy to generate electricity. The first such project began in Hengbung village, Manipur, in July 2022.

## India's First Round-the-Clock Solar-Powered Village

If you make a trip to Modhera village in Gujarat, you will find a solar panel on most roofs. All these panels are linked to a solar power plant and a battery that can store solar power. Throughout the day, the panels produce solar electricity. This is usually much more than what individual homes and buildings need. So, the extra supply is stored in the battery. Once the sun sets, the battery kicks into action, powering the village with stored electricity!

On 9 October 2022, Modhera was declared the first village in India to have round-the-clock solar power. The electrification cost a whopping 80 crore rupees, and the bill was split between the central and state governments. While the project has been a milestone in India's development of solar power, more needs to be done to reduce costs.

Finally, it's also worth noting that while solar and wind energy are far more environmentally friendly than fossil fuels, they are not entirely devoid of environmental impacts. Solar panels (when fixed on the ground) and wind farms take up large plots of land, often getting in the way of humans as well as wildlife in a densely populated country like India. Farmers complain of loss in grazing pastures for their animals, and many birds are killed by wind turbines. The critically endangered Great Indian Bustard has been particularly threatened by wind turbines and power lines that have taken over its habitats in Rajasthan and Gujarat.

The noise, especially from wind farms, has also been known to cause sleeplessness, headaches and irritability in people living close to them. Moreover, the equipment used to generate solar and wind power is made up of materials such as plastic, metal and fibreglass, many of which are mined from the earth and are non-biodegradable. So, when such equipment is damaged or no longer usable, it ends up as hard-to-recycle e-waste.

Nevertheless, in a country where the need for electricity has been rising swiftly, and peak demand has crossed 200 gigawatts, producing renewable power will go a long way in controlling air pollution.

## More Ways in Which Technology Is Helping India's Natural Environment

During the 1990s, conservation scientist Dr Ullas Karanth pioneered the use of camera traps—cameras with motion sensors mounted on tree trunks or poles—to study the population of leopards and tigers at the Nagarhole National Park in Karnataka. Since then, the use of camera traps has increased, providing rich insights into life inside India's wild places—the different kinds of animals found within them, animal behaviour and the impact of human activities. Camera traps have been a boon for wildlife research in the country, paving the way for other useful technologies, such as radio tags and collars that are placed on individual animals to track their movements.

Can you find out about other such technologies?

..........................................................

..........................................................

..........................................................

..........................................................

..........................................................

..........................................................

..........................................................

..........................................................

..........................................................

..........................................................

..........................................................

..........................................................

..........................................................

..........................................................

..........................................................

# Living with Intelligent Machines

The human brain is a marvellous organ. Packed with billions of interconnected nerve cells or neurons, it is so complex that scientists are yet to fully understand exactly how it works and makes us capable of what is called 'human intelligence'. Thinking, reasoning, remembering, understanding, learning and creating . . . human intelligence gives us an astonishing range of capabilities.

With the coming of the first computers in the wake of World War II, an idea began going around in scientific circles in the US—could machines be made as intelligent as humans? In the 1950s, the American computer scientist John McCarthy coined the term 'Artificial Intelligence' (AI) to describe the science and engineering behind intelligent machines, especially intelligent computer programs. The idea generated both fascination and fear, as captured in numerous books, TV series and movies where intelligent machines take control of human lives. Yet, turning AI into reality has been one of the toughest challenges in technological history.

## The Human Brain and AI

Our brain is made up of 100 billion interconnected neurons forming an enormous neural network. Any information entering the brain is processed by this network, helping us learn, remember useful things, solve problems and make decisions. Soon after the first computers were invented, computer scientists began to wonder if there was a way these machines could process the information (data) being entered into them like the human brain to learn, think and make decisions. This simple idea inspired the development of Artificial Intelligence (AI). However, it took a long time for computers to have enough memory and processing power to match the capabilities of the human brain.

Learning is a key to our intelligence. Our brain is constantly learning from all the information that it processes. Similarly, at the heart of AI is machine learning—the ability of machines to learn from all the data fed into them. However, the way machines learn is very different from the way we do. Humans learn through understanding, experiences, emotions, seeing patterns and generalizing. There is no precise formula to our learning. Machines, on the other hand, require lots of data and a clear set of rules or algorithms, instructing them what to do.

Advances in machine learning have brought AI close to mimicking many abilities of human intelligence, such as mastering a specific field of knowledge, playing games that require advanced levels of problem-solving, holding a conversation in a human language, recognizing and copying a user's voice and even generating art!

## Training a Machine

If you want a machine to learn how to identify elephants in photos, you will first need to provide it with thousands of pictures as data because, unlike a human, it hasn't actually 'seen' an elephant.

Once this data has been entered, you will need to instruct the machine: 'this is an elephant' or 'this is not an elephant'. Machines also learn from mistakes. For example, every time you point out to your machine that it has wrongly identified an elephant, it corrects itself.

Machines lack emotions. This means that if you feed in a picture of an elephant in a clown costume, your machine will not laugh raucously. Instead, it will get confused and will need to be instructed that it's seeing an elephant.

As your machine processes more and more pictures, it begins to spot patterns, such as the shape and size of the trunk and the ears, that help it to identify elephants. Interconnected networks, like the neural network in our brain, play an important role in helping machines spot these patterns. The more advanced the network, the more capable your machine.

After it has been through this exercise enough number of times, your machine will become a highly skilled elephant spotter. Machines are very good at learning specific tasks because, unlike humans, they can practise continuously without getting distracted by things happening around them.

What they're yet to do skilfully is switching easily from one task to another. Your elephant-spotting machine, for example, will need to be re-trained if you want it to spot dogs.

## Timeline: From The Imitation Game to ChatGPT

**1950:** English mathematician Alan Turing published a research paper called *Computing Machinery and Intelligence* which began by posing the question: 'Can machines think?'. The paper went on to propose a test to determine whether a machine was *actually* thinking. It called this test 'The Imitation Game' because it essentially evaluated how accurately a computer could imitate human intelligence to make users believe that they were interacting with a person instead of a machine.

Alan Turing

**1956:** At a landmark conference at Dartmouth University in the USA, a group of scientists led by John McCarthy investigated the possibility of creating thinking machines. Over the following decade (1960s–1970s), scientists began testing various inventions that displayed different types of 'intelligent' behaviour, laying the foundations of modern AI. However, most of these inventions were restricted by the computer technology of the time, which wasn't sufficiently advanced to support the complex programming required for AI.

**1959:** The first AI laboratory opened at Massachusetts Institute of Technology (MIT) in the USA.

**1960:** John McCarthy developed LISP, a programming language for AI that was used by developers for decades. Many found it rather bizarre because of its overuse of parentheses (round brackets like these) and joked that its full form was '**L**ots of **I**rrelevant **S**illy **P**arentheses'.

**1966:** Computer scientist Joseph Weizenbaum at MIT's AI Laboratory invented ELIZA, widely regarded as the first chatbot—a computer program that can imitate human conversation. Many users were struck by its capability and spent hours chatting with it.

**1971:** The real world is full of bewildering details, and it's easy for AI developers to forget about some of these. One way around this was to develop programs capable of intelligent behaviour within simulated environments called microworlds. The Blocks World was one such microworld. As the name suggests, it contained coloured blocks, boxes and pyramids in different shapes and sizes strewn on a flat surface. Among the most acclaimed AI programs in the Blocks World was the oddly named SHRDLU, which controlled a robot arm that could rearrange the blocks. Developed by Terry Winograd, a PhD student at Stanford University, in 1971, one of SHRDLU's most lauded features was its ability to take instructions and give feedback to its users in English.

**1972:** Humans need a long time and tremendous amounts of learning to become experts in any field of knowledge.

Was it possible to train machines to acquire such expertise? This was what many researchers were exploring during the 1970s and 1980s. These expert systems were populated with all the information about some narrow field of knowledge that an expert or a group of experts would have. So, a good expert system could work with human experts and even outperform them.

One of the early successes was MYCIN, an expert system developed at Stanford University in 1972 that specialized in blood diseases. Over a period of five years, a team of developers and medical experts at the university encoded MYCIN with expert-level knowledge about blood diseases. Eventually, the program was able to diagnose these diseases, explain how it had arrived at its diagnosis, answer questions related to this and also cope with information that wasn't entirely certain. In the trials carried out in 1979, its abilities surpassed general practitioners and matched the level of human experts in ten real cases of blood diseases that it diagnosed.

**1980s:** Human intelligence works within the real world, but would AI be able to do this? Australian roboticist Rodney Brooks led a strident critique on how AI had been turned into a laboratory experiment, heavy on knowledge but separated from the living world. His criticism generated much debate and laid the foundation for behavioural AI—intelligence as expressed through visible behaviour within a real environment. A famous example of such AI was an 'intelligent' robot

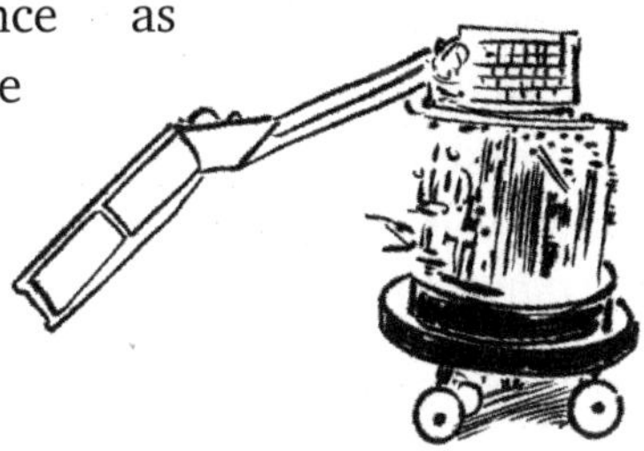

Herbert the bot

designed by Brooks that searched for and cleared empty soda cans from desks and tables at the MIT AI Laboratory and placed them in the recycle bin. It was fondly called Herbert, after the AI pioneer Herbert Simon.

**1990s:** Behavioural AI inspired the development of 'agents'—AI systems that could actively work with human users and help them carry out specific tasks. Yet, it would take years before such agents became a practical reality (hint: see 2011!).

Many of us enjoy playing board games such as chess. Playing such games requires problem-solving and planning skills, signalling intelligence. It took a long time for AI to match humans at this, but in 1997, IBM made headlines when its AI system Deep Blue was able to beat the world chess champion, Garry Kasparov.

Garry Kasparov playing against Deep Blue

**2011:** IBM's Watson computer defeated Ken Jennings and Brad Rutter in a special edition of the American television game show *Jeopardy!* The machine's ability to understand and answer questions posed in natural (human) language marked a leap in AI's ability to process such languages.

Meanwhile, all the work on agents during the 1990s led to the creation of AI-powered virtual assistants. The first of these was Siri. Initially offered in 2010 as an app on Apple's mobile operating system, Siri was introduced as the 'coolest feature' in Apple's iPhone 4S that was launched in 2011. Users could ask Siri to carry out various tasks for them, such as playing a song, making a phone call, providing navigation, setting an alarm and so on. Soon, other technology companies were releasing similar virtual assistants.

**2012:** Amazon kickstarted a robotics revolution after it purchased Kiva Systems, a leading robotics company, and put thousands of robots to work in its warehouses.

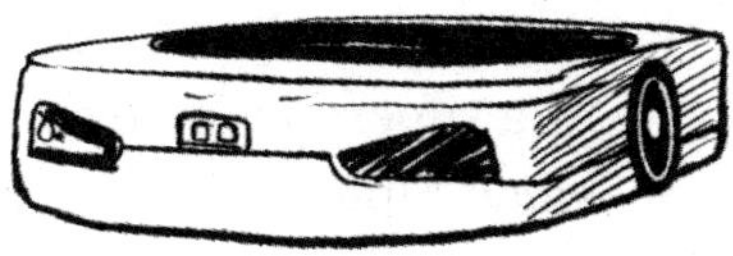

Here's Titan, one of the many robots deployed by Amazon. It transports large and bulky items in the warehouse.

**2014:** Business interest in AI exploded when Google acquired DeepMind, a small UK-based AI start-up that few people had heard of, for 650 million dollars! Everyone was curious to know what DeepMind was doing.

The core technology behind DeepMind was deep learning—a form of machine learning that got much closer to copying the human brain's ability to learn and evolve. Deep learning programs could process complex tasks, such as detecting objects, translating documents, transcribing a sound file into text, that had long needed human intelligence.

**2016:** AlphaGo, an AI system developed by DeepMind, defeated world champion Lee Sedol at the extremely complicated ancient Chinese board game called Go. What separated this achievement from Deep Blue's victory in

1997 was that AlphaGo had taught itself to play the game! How had it managed this? By playing the game repeatedly, experimenting with its moves and learning which ones worked and which didn't. In fact, the commentators in the match between AlphaGo and Lee Sedol did remark on how some of its moves were highly unusual.

This was just the beginning of DeepMind's claim to fame. Eighteen months after this famous victory, it developed AlphaGo Zero, which learned how to play Go at a superhuman level by playing against itself! And then came AlphaZero, which mastered other games.

**2018:** Deep learning had made AI very good at recognizing things, but the results were less impressive when it came to creating new things—new text, images and art. Doing this needed imagination, which AI still did not possess. In 2014, Ian Goodfellow, a researcher at DeepMind, found a way of doing this. He created Generative Adversarial Networks (GANs), a type of machine learning technique that allowed AI to acquire something close to an imagination.

Instead of a single algorithm, GANs use two: a generator and a discriminator. As you may be able to tell by their names, these algorithms are adversaries. The generator generates data that is fake, and the discriminator checks this data against real data to determine if its real or fake. The generator keeps generating and the discriminator keeps identifying the fakes. This process continues till the generator generates something which is fake but matches real data so closely that the discriminator passes it. By doing this, the GAN gets AI to create something new which looks real but doesn't actually exist.

Although this is a truly impressive achievement, it has been put to such unfortunate use that in 2018, such creations made using AI were labelled 'deepfakes'.

**2022:** OpenAI, an American AI research organization rolled out Version 3.5 of ChatGPT—an AI chatbot that had a tremendous ability to learn and communicate like humans—to the public for the very first time. All one needed to do was get on to https://chatgpt.com/ and type in requests in English. Soon afterwards, the chatbot was going viral on social media with awestruck users sharing stories about its incredible abilities. From helping them make travel plans and write speeches to coding computer programs and composing poems—there seemed to be no end to what ChatGPT was capable of. Although AI chatbots had been around for a while, none of them had been as startlingly versatile and effective. Many experts called ChatGPT a tipping point in the history of AI. It made AI leap out decisively from the realm of science fiction and become accessible to anyone with an Internet connection and relevant language skills.

**2023:** Like any AI, even ChatGPT learns using massive amounts of data. But where does this data come from? It comes from pre-existing, human-created work. Naturally, this does not bode well for the human creators who probably spent a long time toiling over their creations, only for a chatbot to conveniently exploit their work without any credit or compensation. In September 2023, a group of authors, including George R.R. Martin, John Grisham and Jodi Picoult, sued OpenAI for 'systematic theft on a mass scale', and in December, the *New York Times* did the same. Such cases left the creators of ChatGPT scrambling for ways to make their creation fairer to human creators whose work the AI borrows from.

**2025:** The Chinese company DeepSeek sent shockwaves through the tech industry when it created an AI model similar to ChatGPT for a fraction of the cost.

## AI in India

In India, AI took root in computer education that had been pioneered at IIT Kanpur during the 1960s. The first course related to it is widely credited to Professor H.N. Mahabala, who mentored some of the biggest names in Indian Information Technology (IT), including Infosys founders Kris Gopalakrishnan and N.R. Narayana Murthy. Predictably, AI's journey mirrored the journey of computers in the country, and it wasn't until the 1980s—when computing was widely promoted by Prime Minister Rajiv Gandhi—that it found greater interest.

Rajiv Gandhi was keen on applying technology to solve various problems faced by India. In 1986, with UN support, his government launched the Knowledge Based Computer Systems (KBCS) project, which marked India's official entry into AI research and laid the foundation for future projects. KBCS wanted to equip computers with human-like expertise in specific areas, such as agriculture, healthcare and education and use them for data-based decision-making. For example, AI systems with expert knowledge of crop diseases could help diagnose these and recommend treatments.

The growth of IT in India during the 2000s expanded the development of AI. Big IT firms like Tata Consultancy Services, Infosys and Wipro began investing in it, and courses related to AI increased to meet the growing demand.

By 2010, technology had streamed into the lives of ordinary Indians like never before. The electronic device at the centre of this transformation was the Internet-enabled smartphone, which could be put to various uses—from calling a contact to watching videos and listening to music. To boost this growing use of technology, the government launched a Digital India Campaign in 2015 to improve Internet connectivity across the country.

As the number of Internet users grew, a flood of data began gushing in, creating a wide variety of opportunities for AI applications. By 2018, the government had put in place a National Strategy for AI (NSAI). At the heart of this strategy lay a simple idea—how could India use AI to promote social welfare without compromising the safety of users?

## What AI for Social Welfare Can Look Like

In 2021, thousands of farmers in the Khammam district of Telangana began using an AI-powered WhatsApp chatbot that was fluent in their language, Telugu, to grow chillies. Over the course of eighteen months, the chatbot offered insights into soil health, recommended fertilizers, identified defects and assessed the quality of the crop. Known as Saagu Baagu, this groundbreaking AI project, launched by the Government of Telangana in association with various organizations working in technology and agriculture, led to a 21 per cent increase in plant growth per acre, reduced pesticide and fertilizer usage and increased sale prices. The success of the project prompted the Telangana government to expand it to lakhs of farmers.

* * *

Between 2020 and 2021, the world was in the grip of the deadly COVID-19 pandemic. An invisible virus was on the prowl, infecting people and claiming many lives. To control the spread of the virus, India imposed social-distancing measures, including two nationwide lockdowns, which confined people to their homes. The use of AI-based systems in healthcare expanded rapidly during this period. MyGov Saathi, an AI chatbot, was created to provide accurate, useful and up-to-date information on COVID-19. Similarly, the Centre for Artificial Intelligence and Robotics developed Atman AI, a software that can detect Covid infections using chest X-rays uploaded to it.

Can you find other ways in which AI is being used for social welfare in India?

While the NSAI gave a major boost to the development of AI in India, what truly shot AI into the imagination of ordinary Indians was ChatGPT. Within a few months of its launch in 2022, lakhs of Indians were reportedly using the chatbot for everything from content creation to coding assistance. At the beginning of 2024, surveys reported that India had the second highest number of ChatGPT users worldwide after the US. Despite its soaring popularity, the development of AI in India faces some significant challenges and poses some grave concerns.

## Lost in Translation

In a multilingual country like India, that has twenty-two official languages and thousands of other dialects, data in many regional languages remains scarce. Without sufficient and good-quality data, the accuracy of AI systems will suffer.

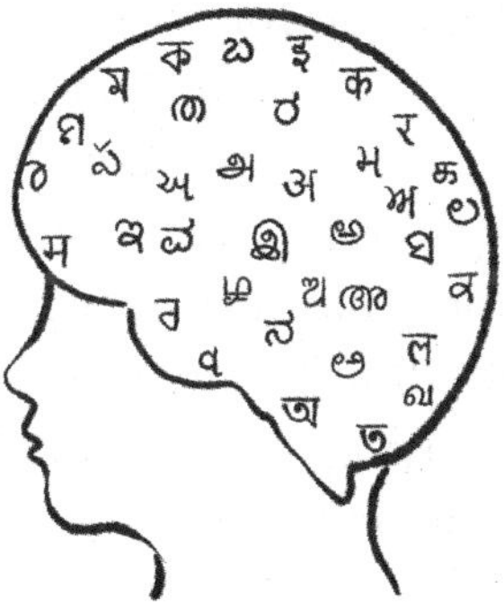

One of the big problems associated with AI programs is bias—making unfair decisions or mistakes because they have not been trained with the right or complete data. In 2015, for example, Amazon found that its AI-based recruitment program was discriminating against women while reviewing resumes for software developer jobs and other technical posts. This happened because it had been trained using resumes submitted to the company over a ten-year period—most of which belonged to men. Having observed this pattern, the program taught itself that male candidates were preferable! Similarly, in 2019, the city of San Francisco banned AI-based facial recognition technology that misidentified people of colour and women because it had been mostly trained using white male faces.

To avoid such problems that arise from inadequate data, India has been actively promoting the use of AI for language translations that can help collect data in different Indian languages. In August 2022, the government launched Bhashini—Bhasha Interface for India—an AI-driven tool that can translate written and spoken text into multiple languages, allowing people to access the Internet and various digital services in their preferred language. In December 2023, Prime Minister Narendra Modi used Bhashini for the first time during a speech he gave at the Kashi Tamil Sangamam in Varanasi. Even though he spoke in Hindi, the audience had the option of listening to his speech in Tamil using live translation by Bhashini. Similar tools are also being developed by other initiatives, such as Project Vaani by the AI and Robotics Technology Park in Bengaluru, the Indian Institute of Science (IISc) and Google India.

## Technical Difficulties

Even as the government collects more data in Indian languages to build richer data sets for AI, it also needs to enhance the country's computing power. Although India has made rapid strides in computing since the 1980s, its capabilities need to be boosted to develop advanced AI systems.

In 2024, the government announced the IndiaAI Mission, under which it set aside 10,000 crore rupees to develop advanced AI systems in the country. At the moment, India lacks the technological capability to manufacture computer chips needed to build such systems, so a big chunk of the funds will go towards buying these. However, the government also hopes to develop India's ability to make such chips on its own (*also see page 101*). Apart from this, the government is investing heavily in creating data centres to store the vast amounts of data needed to train AI systems within the country.

## Handling Misuse

One of the biggest problems associated with AI systems has been their misuse. Some of the earliest complaints came from educators who were worried about students using the technology for school and college work instead of applying their minds. This led to a raging debate. Many educators wanted AI to be banned in schools and colleges. Others encouraged its use to support learning. In a world where AI is becoming all-pervasive, the National Education Policy (NEP) announced by the Indian government in 2020 encourages the use of AI in education.

More worryingly, AI is increasingly being used to commit cybercrimes, such as voice scams. AI has advanced to a point where it only needs to listen to someone's voice for a few seconds to copy it extremely accurately. Such mimicry, a kind of deepfake, may seem amusing, except that cybercriminals are using it to fool people into believing that their family members or friends are in trouble and need money urgently. A 2023 survey found that 47 per cent of Indians have either experienced or know someone who has experienced some kind of an AI voice scam, which was much more than the global average of 25 per cent. About 83 per cent of the victims in India reportedly lost more than 50,000 rupees to such fraudulent calls.

So, what do you do if you get an urgent call from a person close to you, worriedly asking for money because they have been robbed, have met with an accident or have lost their phone or wallet? Hard as it may seem, the first thing to do is not to panic but keep your wits about you, particularly if the person is calling you from an unknown number and is demanding money urgently. There is a high chance that you're being scammed. Install a caller ID on your phone so you can be alerted about the identity and location of a caller and avoid picking up unknown numbers. It may also help to pay attention to code words. AI may clone someone's voice, but it will not know, for example, how they address you. If your name is Radhika and your friends and family usually call you Rads, but the caller is using your complete name and asking for money, disconnect immediately and report the number.

Voice scams are just one of the ways in which AI is being misused by cybercriminals. So, even as the police and cybercrime authorities develop their capabilities to catch cybercriminals, the need for people to get more vigilant has become greater than ever.

## Future Wise

There is no denying that our lives have become increasingly entwined with technology that is capable of matching and, at times, even surpassing human intelligence. What impact will this have on our lives? A big worry for many people is: will AI take away my job?

Every technological revolution in history has created such fears. When computers were first introduced in Indian workplaces during the 1960s, protests broke out on the streets against these 'job-eating' machines. Yet, by the 1990s, the boom in IT had pushed more and more Indians towards pursuing careers in computing.

Today, AI is causing such fears. World organizations, such as the International Monetary Fund, have warned that AI will affect 40 per cent of the jobs globally and will make many of them disappear. However, that's just one side of the story. The other side is that it will also create several new jobs. What this means is that people who have the skills to work with AI will continue to be in demand. But what of the rest?

Currently, the literacy rate in India is around 77 per cent. While this is a huge improvement from what it was at the time of Independence, it also means that more than 20 per cent Indians still don't know how to read and write. Moreover, surveys have found that a majority of India's households don't even have one member who is able to use digital technology effectively. Unless digital literacy improves, many Indians will fall behind even as the country marches ahead on the road to technological modernity.

If history has shown us anything, it is that India's greatest asset is its people—curious, resilient and eager to build a better future. The true measure of its progress will not be in the technologies it develops but in how these technologies empower all its people and not just a fortunate few. Herein lies one of the greatest challenges and biggest opportunities facing India's quest for technological advancement.

# A Technological Timeline of Independent India

## 1947–1949

**1948**: The Atomic Energy Commission is established, beginning India's quest for nuclear power; First multipurpose dam project launched on the Damodar River flowing through the states of West Bengal and present-day Jharkhand; First vaccine laboratory in independent India set up in Madras (now Chennai) to manufacture the BCG vaccine for tuberculosis

## 1950–1959

**1951**: India launches its first five-year plan for national development. It emphasizes scientific and industrial research. (These plans are discontinued in 2017, and the NITI Aayog or the National Institution for Transforming India replaces the Planning Commission to develop more long-term plans and strategies); First Indian Institute of Technology founded in Kharagpur, West Bengal

**1953**: The Indian Statistical Institute (ISI) in Calcutta (now Kolkata) builds India's first analogue computer

**1954**: Hindustan Antibiotics Limited in Maharashtra becomes the first factory in the developing world to manufacture critical medicines

**1955**: The Kaira District Co-operative Milk Producer's Union Limited (now known as AMUL) inaugurates India's first milk powder plant. It is the first time in India's history that ordinary dairy farmers own the country's most technologically advanced dairy—the first in the world to mass-produce milk powder from buffalo milk

**1956**: India begins developing its first fighter jet—HF-24 Marut—but it is plagued by engine troubles and doesn't live up to expectations

**1958**: The Defence Research and Development Organisation (DRDO) is established to develop advanced defence technology; Transistor radios introduce Indians to the joys of portable electronics

**1960–1969**

**1960**: The first agricultural university in independent India—G.B. Pant University of Agriculture and Technology—is founded in Uttarakhand (then part of Uttar Pradesh); The Tata Institute of Fundamental Research in Mumbai builds India's first digital computer, TIFRAC. (In 1971, it is manufactured and marketed as the Trombay Digital Computer 12 or TDC-12 by ECIL.)

**1961**: Esso Standard Eastern in Mumbai becomes the first company in India to install a computer in its office—an IBM 1401

**1962**: The Indian National Committee for Space Research (INCOSPAR) is established to develop space technology. It is eventually called the Indian Space Research Organisation (ISRO); Bharat Electronics Limited (BEL) sets up a fab to manufacture semiconductors—a crucial electronic component—in India. (It loses out to higher-quality, cheaper imports from China, Taiwan and South Korea during the 1980s. Various other attempts are made to restart indigenous semiconductor manufacturing, but they all fall short.)

**1963**: First sounding rocket is launched from Thumba in Kerala, marking India's entry into the Space Age; First instant food mixes for idlis, gulab jamuns and jalebis are manufactured and marketed in India. Although slow to take off, highly processed food products go on to revolutionize Indian kitchens by reducing time and effort required for cooking; The DRDO completes the prototype of the first indigenous battle tank—Vijayanta. It is handed over to the army in 1965, after further tests, adjustments and improvements

**1966**: The Green Revolution powered by scientifically developed high-yielding seeds, chemical fertilizers and pesticides, advanced irrigation and farm machines helps India fight hunger and eventually export food grains

**1967**: First Earth Station—ground infrastructure connecting Earth to satellites in space—opens in Ahmedabad; First indigenous sounding rocket—Rohini 75—is launched from Thumba

**1968**: Tata Consultancy Services (TCS), widely considered the first Indian IT company, is established in Mumbai. In the coming decades, India builds a world-renowned IT industry

**1969**: Asia's first commercial nuclear power plant comes up at Tarapur in Maharashtra

## 1970–1979

**1970**: The Milk Revolution begins in India. The spread of advanced dairying transforms the country into a leading milk producer; Oral Polio Vaccine is developed and produced in India. It plays a key role in India's battle against polio

**1972**: IIT Kanpur introduces the first postgraduate programmes in computer science

**1974**: India tests its first nuclear bomb. (In 1998, after testing five more bombs, it declares itself a nuclear-weapon state.); First indigenous tractor—Swaraj—is launched in India. The growing popularity of tractors paves the way for other indigenous tractor-operated machinery in Indian farms

**1975**: The first indigenous satellite, Aryabhata, is launched from the USSR; Satellite Instructional Television Experiment (SITE)—the first major use of technology for education—is launched across six states

**1977**: The first FM Radio Station is launched by the government in Madras. FM offers a better listening experience and slowly begins to replace the AM radio transmission that existed in India from before Independence

**1979**: The Electronics Corporation of India (ECIL) develops a working model of an Electronic Voting Machine (EVM). It is approved, and in 1980, both ECIL and BEL begin to manufacture it

## 1980–1989

**1980**: India becomes the sixth nation in the world to design, build and launch satellites, after its Satellite Launch Vehicle (SLV 3) successfully places the indigenous satellite Rohini 1 into space

**1982**: India's first communication and meteorology satellite, INSAT-1A, is launched by the US, followed by INSAT-1B the next year. These satellites revolutionize television and radio by enabling long-distance broadcasts. Soon afterwards, India gets its first taste of colour television; Veterinarian and poultry businessman, Banda Vasudev Rao, establishes the National Egg Coordination Committee, a cooperative of egg farmers, that leads to an egg revolution in India by popularizing modern poultry farming techniques, battling shortages and aggressively marketing eggs to Indian consumers

**1983**: Rakesh Sharma becomes the first Indian to travel to space; India establishes Dakshin Gangotri, its first permanent research station in Antarctica; The DRDO begins the Integrated Missile Development Programme (IGMDP) to develop strategic indigenous missiles

**1984**: The first metro rail system is introduced in Kolkata. It connects Dum Dum and Tollygunge and is completely underground. (Delhi Metro follows in 2002); The Centre for Development of Telematics (C-DOT) begins developing reliable, rugged and cost-effective digital switches for better telephone connectivity in India. Launched in 1986, C-DOT puts a large number of villages on the telephone network for the very first time and ushers in a telecom revolution

**1985**: Computerization of ticket reservations by Indian Railways takes computers into India's public life in a significant way. Eventually, banking, stock trading and several other public services are computerized; The Blue Revolution is launched to develop, manage and promote aquatic produce, such as fish, shrimp and prawn

**1988**: India launches its first successful ballistic missile—Prithvi-I. The missile is inducted into the armed forces in 1994, following further tests, adjustments and improvements; India's first remote sensing satellite, IRS-1A, is launched by the Soviet Union. Remote sensing plays an important role in helping India monitor the natural resources spread over its vast territory; Scientists at the Council of Scientific and Industrial Research (CSIR) and Centre for Cellular and Molecular Biology (CCMB) develop a DNA fingerprinting probe, making India the third country to possess this technology. The probe is used in investigating crime scenes and identifying suspects

**1989**: India launches its first nuclear-capable ballistic missile—Agni-I. It is inducted into the armed forces in 2007

and leads to the development of India's most significant set of indigenous missiles

**1990–1999**

**1991**: Groundbreaking economic reforms impact all walks of Indian life, including technology; India's first supercomputer—PARAM 8000—is developed by the Centre for Development of Advanced Computing (C-DAC). The initiative is led by computer scientist Vijay Pandurang Bhatkar

**1995**: Public launch of the Internet and mobile phone marks the beginning of a digital revolution in India

**1996**: IndiaMART becomes the first major e-commerce platform founded in India

**1997**: The ICICI Bank begins online banking in India

**1998**: Tata launches Indica—the first truly indigenous car (nearly 98 per cent of its parts are designed and manufactured locally)

**2000–2009**

**2000**: The millennium bug, also called the Y2K (Year 2000) problem, creates a huge demand for Indian programmers in the West and plays a pivotal role in boosting India's software industry; Major Internet platforms like Yahoo!, MSN and eBay begin their India portals, paving the way for others like Google and Amazon; Railway reservations start getting offered online (airlines follow two years later); The government passes the Information Technology Act—the first cyber law of the country

**2001**: The BrahMos, one of fastest cruise missiles in the world, is successfully launched. Developed under a secret accord with Russia, it goes on to significantly boost India's defence exports; India successfully develops its first fighter jet—Tejas—which is handed over to the air force in 2016, following further tests, adjustments and improvements

**2002**: The government allows the cultivation of genetically modified Bt Cotton. This sets off a biotechnology revolution in the country and makes India one of the world's largest producers and exporters of cotton. However, it also leads to a raging debate on the use of genetically engineered seeds

**2004**: Broadband Internet is introduced in India; The number of mobile phones surpasses the number of landlines in India

**2005**: Online social networking begins in India with the launch of the social media platform Orkut by Google; Motorola C115 becomes the first made-in-India mobile phone

**2006**: India announces its first e-governance plan to make various government services available online

**2008**: Chandrayaan-1, India's first moon mission, reaches the moon; Launch of the 3G network revolutionizes mobile connectivity, marking a major shift from primarily voice-based communication to a more accessible and faster mobile Internet experience. This continues to improve with the introduction of 4G and eventually 5G networks in successive years; Reliance Entertainment launches BIGFlix, India's first OTT platform (a digital platform to browse and watch videos online)

**2009**: The DRDO launches INS *Arihant*—the first indigenous nuclear submarine. It is inducted into the navy in 2016, following further tests, adjustments and improvements, and completes the nuclear triad—India's ability to launch nuclear strikes from land, air and underwater

## 2010–2019

**2010**: Aadhaar—the world's largest identity project—is launched in India. It issues a twelve-digit unique identification number based on biometric data and becomes the basis for India Stack—a set of government-backed digital tools that allow people to do a number of things online, such as sign documents (eSign) and store copies of important identity proofs and other documents in a digital locker (DigiLocker)

**2012**: The Golden Quadrilateral—India's most extensive highway project connecting Delhi, Mumbai, Chennai and Kolkata—is completed.

**2013**: India's first satellite dedicated to military use—GSAT-7—is launched by the European Space Agency; First navigation satellite—IRNSS-1A—is launched by ISRO;

The National Power Grid is completed, linking producers and consumers of electricity across the country

**2014**: India becomes the first country to land a spacecraft on Mars in its very first attempt; Pradhan Mantri Jan Dhan Yojana (prime minister's people's money scheme) takes banking to crores of Indians for the very first time

**2015**: The government announces the Digital India Campaign to improve Internet connectivity in India

**2016**: Unified Payments Interface (UPI), a digital payment system is launched under India Stack. It revolutionizes digital payments by making it possible for people to send and receive money using their mobile phones; Reliance Jio disrupts the telecom market with extremely cheap mobile services

**2017**: ISRO breaks a space record by successfully launching 104 satellites together

**2018**: India announces Gaganyaan—the first mission to carry an Indian crew into space; Indian Railways flags off Vande Bharat—the first trainset designed and built in the country

## 2020 and Beyond

**2020**: COVID-19 pandemic restricts Indians to their homes, leading to an unprecedented surge in the use of digital technologies; The first Kisan Rail from Devlali in Maharashtra to Danapur in Bihar marks a major milestone in cold storage development in India, reducing agricultural waste and enhancing the supply of perishable fruits and vegetables across the country

**2021**: The government announces a Semiconductor Mission under which it lays the foundation for establishing three semiconductor factories—a facility in Dholera, Gujarat, and two assembly, testing, marking and packaging facilities in Sanand, Gujarat, and Morigaon, Assam. (The first semiconductor chip from Dholera is expected to roll out by the end of 2026, marking a significant milestone for India's electronics industry that continues to rely heavily on imports.)

**2022**: Public launch of ChatGPT Version 3.5 catapults Artificial Intelligence (AI) into people's lives like never before. By 2024, India has the second largest number of users.

**2024**: Aditya-L1, India's first mission to study the sun, reaches the point in space from where it will be able to continuously watch the sun; The government announces IndiaAI Mission and sets aside 10,000 crore rupees to develop AI systems in India

# Acknowledgements

I've spent the past eight years of my life researching and writing books chronicling various histories of independent India for young and lay readers. It's been as exhausting as it's been rewarding. But attempting to write a technological history has by far been the most complicated and intimidating undertaking, and I owe a tremendous debt of gratitude to innumerable people who have helped me on this journey.

To writers and historians who have created the relatively modest yet magnificent body of work on this theme, especially Dinesh C. Sharma and Arun Mohan Sukumar. Not to forget, all the journalists who have covered technological development comprehensively in their reportage. This book owes a lot to you.

Sohini Mitra, I'll be forever grateful for your unwavering trust in me.

Sayan Mukherjee, thank you for agreeing to illustrate yet another book in this series.

Vinayak Varma, Samar Bansal, Shabari Choudhury, Mansi Dhanraj Shetty, Binita Roy, Kafeel Ahmad and the entire team at Penguin Random House India for bringing this book to life—may it be long and fruitful.

Srinath Perur and Richa Chadda, thank you for generously offering to review a raw and overlong draft of this book. I have benefitted greatly from your thoughtful comments and encouragement.

Arvind Sardana, Devika Cariapa, Chitrajit Cariapa, Dr P.J. Bhat, Manash Chatterjee, Deeptha Vivekanand, Meena Agarwal, Aditi Patil, Shubham Goel, Radhika Agarwal, Rubin D' Cruz, Nandini Nayar, Archana Atri, Richa Jha, Manasa Gade and Vidya Mani for your help in reviewing different parts of this book.

Raghunath Mashelkar, Rakesh Sharma, Rahul Sharma, O.P. Agarwal, Ankit Agrawal, Apar Gupta, Shreya Singhal and Nidesh Soni, your stories have given much perspective to this narrative.

Srijan Pal Singh, Charles Assisi and Dinesh C. Sharma, I'm grateful to you for the foreword and the endorsements.

Harini Nagendra and Shashwat DC at the Nature Writing for Children Programme and Dr Alexia Casale, my partner on the Literature across Borders project—thank you so much for all your kindness and support.

Radhika Menon, much of what I know about a good children's book comes from my years with Tulika Publishers.

My friends and well-wishers, I feel incredibly blessed to have you in my life.

Booksellers, librarians, readers and reviewers, who have backed my adventures in writing and kept me going—thank you!

My family—Dad, Bhai, Melody—and most of all my mother, my first reader, fair critic and fervent supporter—I love you very much and am here because of you.

# Selected Bibliography

## Books

Agrawal, Ravi. *India Connected: How the Smartphone Is Transforming the World's Largest Democracy.* Oxford University Press, 2018.

Ahluwalia, Montek Singh. *Backstage: The Story Behind India's High Growth Years*. New Delhi: Rupa Publications, 2020.

Amir, Sayed Mohammad. *A Career in Radio: Understanding the Key Building Blocks*. Abingdon and New York: Routledge, 2024.

Bhalla, G.S. *Indian Agriculture since Independence*. New Delhi: National Book Trust, 2007.

Bhatia, Rahul. *The Identity Project: The Unmaking of a Democracy*. Chennai: Westland Books, 2024.

Chowdhry, Ajai. *Just Aspire: Notes on Technology, Entrepreneurship and the Future*. Gurugram: Harper Collins India, 2023.

Guha, Ramachandra. *India after Gandhi: The History of the World's Largest Democracy*. London: Pan Macmillan, 2007.

Jeffrey, Robin, and Assa Doron. *Cell Phone Nation: How Mobile Phones Have Revolutionized Business, Politics and Ordinary Life in India*. Hachette India, 2013.

Kavic, Lorne J. *India's Quest for Security: Defence Policies 1947–1965*. Berkeley: University of California Press, 2023.

Logan, William A.T. *A Technological History of Cold-War India, 1947–1969: Autarky and Foreign Aid*. Switzerland: Palgrave Macmillan, 2022.

Mehta, Nalin. *India's Techade: Digital Revolution and Change in the World's Largest Democracy*. Chennai: Westland Books, 2023.

Menon, Nikhil. *Planning Democracy: How a Professor, an Institute, and an Idea Shaped India.* Gurugram: Penguin Random House India, 2022.

Merrill, Dennis. *Bread and the Ballot: The United States and India's Economic Development, 1947–1963*. University of North Carolina Press, 1990.

Perkovich, George. *India's Nuclear Bomb: The Impact on Global Proliferation*. University of California Press, 1999.

Pitroda, Sam, and David Chanoff. *Dreaming Big: My Journey to Connect India*. Gurugram: Penguin Random House India, 2015.

Sharma, Dinesh C. *Indian Innovation Not Jugaad: 100 Ideas That Transformed India*. New Delhi: Roli Books, 2022.

Sharma, Dinesh C. *The Long Revolution: The Birth and Growth of India's IT Industry*. Harper Collins India, 2009.

Singh, Gurbir. *The Indian Space Programme: India's Incredible Journey from the Third World to the First*. Astrotalkuk Publications, 2017.

Subramaniam, Arjun. *India's Wars: A Military History, 1947–1971*. Gurugram: Harper Collins India, 2016.

Subramaniam, Arjun. *A Military History of India since 1972*. University Press of Kansas, 2021.

Sukumar, Arun Mohan. *Midnight's Machines—A Political History of Technology in India*. Gurugram: Penguin Random House India, 2019.

Ramnath, N.S., and Charles Assisi. *The Aadhaar Effect: Why the World's Largest Identity Project Matters*. Oxford University Press, 2018.

Rao, Sujatha K. *Do We Care? India's Health System*. Oxford University Press, 2017.

Vachharajani, Bijal. *So You Want to Know About the Environment*. New Delhi: Rupa Publications, 2017.

Wooldridge, Michael. *A Brief History of Artificial Intelligence: What It Is, Where We Are, and Where We Are Going*. New York: Flatiron Books, 2021.

Yadav, Sajjan Singh. *India's Vaccine Growth Story: From Cowpox to Vaccine Maitri*. New Delhi: Sage Publications, 2022.

**Other Resources**

'How One Man Fought a Patent War over Turmeric.' Dr Raghunath Mashelkar interview by Alexi Horowitz-Ghazi and Erika Beras. NPR, Planet Money, podcast transcript. 1 September 2023. https://www.npr.org/transcripts/1197321273.

Ganguly, Rajat. 'India's Military: Evolution, Modernisation and Transformation.' *India Quarterly: A Journal of International Affairs* (September 2015).

Senapati, Manas Ranjan, and Ajay Kumar Swain. 'Dr Kalam: The Missile Man of India.' *Odisha Review* (January 2017). https://magazines.odisha.gov.in/Orissareview/2017/Jan/engpdf/37-38.pdf.

Upadhyay, Akshat. 'Fighting Future Wars: Preparing India for Conflicts in the 21st Century.' Observer Research Foundation. *Issue Brief*, no. 525 (March 2022). https://www.orfonline.org/research/fighting-future-wars-preparing-india-for-conflicts-in-the-21st-century.

Kerala Road Safety Authority. 'History of Roads.' http://roadsafety.kerala.gov.in/roads.

Press Information Bureau. 'Year End Review 2023-Ministry of Road Transport and Highways' (press release, Ministry of Road Transport & Highways). https://pib.gov.in/PressReleaseIframePage.aspx?PRID=1993425.

Bhagwati, Jaimini, and Shalini Chauhan. 'Riding the Tracks of Time: Indian Railways—An Unfinished Revolution' (working paper 68, February 2024). Centre for Social and Economic Progress. https://csep.org/wp-content/uploads/2024/02/Riding-the-Track-of-time_Indian-Railways-2.pdf.

Press Information Bureau. 'Infrastructure Expansion in India Witnesses Significant Growth in Recent Years: Economic Survey 2023–24' (press release, Ministry of Finance). https://pib.gov.in/PressReleaseIframePage.aspx?PRID=2034955.

India Post. 'Post Office Network.' https://www.indiapost.gov.in/VAS/Pages/AboutUs/PostOfficeNetwork.aspx.

Central Electricity Authority. 'Growth of Electricity Sector in India from 1947–2024.' https://cea.nic.in/wp-content/uploads/pdm/2024/08/Growth_Book_2024.pdf.

Directorate of Ordnance (Coordination and Services). 'Growth of Indian Ordnance Factories.' https://ddpdoo.gov.in/pages/history#Growth.

Brigadier Defence Academy, 'Strength of the Indian Army in 2023.' https://brigadierdefenceacademy.in/indian-army-strength-in-2023/.

Peri, Dinakar. 'India's Fighter Jet Conundrum.' *The Hindu*. 21 April 2023. https://www.thehindu.com/news/national/indias-fighter-jet-conundrum/article66761396.ece.

'India's Navy Expands Fleet with Eyes on Indian Ocean Rivalry.' *Al Jazeera*. 15 January 2025. https://www.aljazeera.com/news/2025/1/15/indias-navy-expands-fleet-with-eyes-on-indian-ocean-rivalry.

Varma, Vinayak. 'Starman: An Interview with Rakesh Sharma.' *Brainwave* 1, no. 6 (May 2011).

Menon, Vandana, Raghav Bikhchandani, and Humra Laeeq. 'Hungry India, a Nawabi US President, "Mexican Blood"—the Real Story of Green Revolution.' *The Print*. 19 February 2022. https://theprint.in/past-forward/hungry-india-a-nawabi-us-president-mexican-blood-the-real-story-of-green-revolution/835649/.

Kishore, Avinash. 'Why Farmers in India Adopt Certain Technologies but Ignore Others.' International Food Policy Research Institute (IFPRI blog). 6 July 2018. https://www.ifpri.org/blog/why-farmers-india-adopt-certain-technologies-ignore-others/.

Indian Council for Research on International Economic Relations (ICRIER). 'India: The Impact of Mobile Phones,' Moving the debate forward: The Policy Paper series, no. 9. January 2009. https://www.icrier.org/pdf/public_policy19jan09.pdf.

NABARD. 'All India Rural Financial Inclusion Survey 2021-22.' https://www.nabard.org/auth/writereaddata/tender/pub_0910240156351156.pdf.

Swaminathan, R. 'India's Electronics Sector: Policies, Practices and Lessons from China.' Observer Research Foundation. *ORF Occasional Paper*, no. 52 (June 2014). https://www.orfonline.org/research/india-s-electronics-sector-policies-practices-and-lessons-from-china.

Sivaram, Choodie. 'India's Semiconductor Moment.' *The Statesman*. 17 February 2022. Opinion section. https://www.thestatesman.com/opinion/indias-semiconductor-moment-1503046515.html.

Rajaraman, V. 'History of Computing in India: 1955–2010.' *IEEE Annals of the History of Computing* 37, no. 1 (2015): 24–35.

ET Bureau. 'A Telecom Revolution This Decade.' *The Economic Times*. 31 December 2009. Business news section, industry. https://economictimes.indiatimes.com/industry/telecom/a-telecom-revolution-this-decade/articleshow/5397564.cms.

Mansur, Rishabh. '25 Years of Mobile Phones: India's Journey to Becoming World's Second-Largest Smartphone Market.' YourStory. 1 August 2020. https://yourstory.com/2020/07/india-mobile-phones-smartphone-market-25-years.

'India "Beef" Lynching: Local Groups Fanning Anti-Muslim Violence?' *BBC online*. 2 October 2015. https://www.bbc.com/news/world-asia-india-34421417.

George, Nycil. 'CMS Drives Webdunia's Multilingual Portals.' *Firstpost*. 9 October 2007. Business section. https://www.firstpost.com/business/biztech/cms-drives-webdunias-multilingual-portals-1862201.html.

Dhapola, Shruti. 'From Voice to Video, Why Indian Languages Are Again Google's Big Focus.' *The Indian Express*. 26 September

2018. Technology section. https://indianexpress.com/article/technology/tech-news-technology/from-voice-to-video-why-indian-languages-are-again-googles-big-focus-5375419/.

Manral, Mahender Singh, and Jignasa Sinha. '24% Rise in Cybercrime in 2022, 11% Surge in Economic Offences: NCRB report.' *The Indian Express*. 4 December 2023. https://indianexpress.com/article/india/rise-cybercrime-2022-economic-offences-ncrb-report-9053882/.

Mishra, Soni. 'Meet the Team Members Who Conceptualised the EVM.' *The Week*. 7 April 2024. https://www.theweek.in/theweek/current/2024/03/30/meet-the-team-members-who-conceptualised-the-electronic-voting-machine.html.

Debnath, Sisir, Shamika Ravi, and Mudit Kapoor. 'Do Electronic Voting Machines Work for Indian Voters?' *ISB Insight* 6 (17 July 2018). https://isbinsight.isb.edu/do-electronic-voting-machines-work-for-indian-voters/.

Jain, Anushka, and Vrinda Bhandari. 'The Development of Surveillance Technology in India: Beyond Judicial Review or Oversight.' Verfassungsblog. 7 April 2022. https://verfassungsblog.de/os6-india/.

Software Freedom Law Centre. *Living in Digital Darkness: A Handbook on Internet Shutdowns in India*. New Delhi: SFLC.in. 2018. https://sflc.in/wp-content/uploads/2018/05/Living-in-Digital-Darkness-A-Handbook-on-Internet-Shutdowns-in-India-May-2018-by-SFLCin.pdf.

Columbia University, Global Freedom of Expression. 'Bhasin v. Union of India.' https://globalfreedomofexpression.columbia.edu/cases/bhasin-v-union-of-india/.

Columbia University, Global Freedom of Expression. 'Shreya Singhal v. Union of India.' https://globalfreedomofexpression.columbia.edu/cases/shreya-singhal-v-union-of-india/.

Amrith, Sunil S. 'Health in India since Independence.' University of Manchester, Brooks World Poverty Institute. *BWPI Working Paper* 79 (February 2009). https://hummedia.manchester.

ac.uk/institutes/gdi/publications/workingpapers/bwpi/bwpi-wp-7909.pdf.

Kumar, Mohana S. 'Literacy Movement in Kerala: One Step Forward, Two Step Backwards.' *Economic and Political Weekly* 28, no. 41 (9 October 1993): 2187–2191.

Rao, Siriginidi Subba. 'Distance Education and the Role of IT in India.' The Electronic Library 24, no. 2 (March 2006): 225–236. https://www.researchgate.net/publication/220677404_Distance_education_and_the_role_of_IT_in_India.

Mitra, Sugata. 'The Hole in the Wall Project and the Power of Self-Organized Learning (e-book excerpt).' Edutopia. 3 February 2012. https://www.edutopia.org/blog/self-organized-learning-sugata-mitra.

Clark, Donald. 'Mitra–Hole in the Wall . . . but Holes in the Research . . .' Donald Clark Plan B (blog). 6 April 2020. http://donaldclarkplanb.blogspot.com/2020/04/mitra-hole-in-wall-but-holes-in-research.html.

Tyabji, Nasir. 'Gaining Technical Know-How in an Unequal World: Penicillin Manufacture in Nehru's India.' Munich Personal RePEc Archive. April 2004. https://mpra.ub.uni-muenchen.de/84236/.

National Health Mission. 'Immunization.' https://nhm.gov.in/index1.php?lang=1&level=2&sublinkid=824&lid=220.

James, T.C., and Abha Jaiswal. 'Medical Devices Industry in India: Local Manufacturing and Trade.' Research and Information System for Developing Countries. April 2020. https://www.ris.org.in/sites/default/files/Publication/Medical%20Devices_Report.pdf.

Biswas, Debolina. '[Startup Bharat] Telemedicine May Be on the Rise, but Is It Reaching Rural India That Needs It the Most?' YourStory. 11 March 2020. https://yourstory.com/2020/03/startup-bharat-telemedicine-practo-mfine-prime-venture.

Dubey, Divyani. 'Has India Really Achieved WHO Recommended Doctor-Population Ratio?' FactChecker. 3 August 2022. https://

www.factchecker.in/context-check/has-india-really-achieved-who-recommended-doctor-population-ratio-829064.

Thapliyal, Jotirmay. 'RLEK Fought & Won First Environment Case in SC.' *The Tribune*. Last modified on 25 April 2016. https://www.tribuneindia.com/news/archive/courts/rlek-fought-won-first-environment-case-in-sc-227108/.

Kumar, Sumit. 'How New Law in E-Waste Recycling Is Putting Mayapuri Industries in a Scrape.' *The Economic Times*. Last modified on 6 August 2012. https://economictimes.indiatimes.com/north/how-new-law-in-e-waste-recycling-is-putting-mayapuri-industries-in-a scrape/articleshow/15374416.cms.

Baldé, Cornelis P., Ruediger Kuehr, Tales Yamamoto, Rosie McDonald, Elena D'Angelo, Shahana Althaf, Garam Bel, Otmar Deubzer, Elena Fernandez-Cubillo, Vanessa Forti, Vanessa Gray, Sunil Herat, Shunichi Honda, Giulia Iattoni, Deepali S. Khetriwal, Vittoria Luda di Cortemiglia, Yuliya Lobuntsova, Innocent Nnorom, Noémie Pralat, and Michelle Wagner. 'The Global E-Waste Monitor 2024.' International Telecommunication Union (ITU) and United Nations Institute for Training and Research (UNITAR), Geneva/Bonn. 2024. https://ewastemonitor.info/wp-content/uploads/2024/03/GEM_2024_18-03_web_page_per_page_web.pdf.

De Majo, Claudio. 'Italy's Poison Ships: How an International Trade of Hazardous Waste Sparked a Grassroots Struggle for Environmental Justice.' *Arcadia*, no. 44 (autumn 2020). https://www.environmentandsociety.org/arcadia/italys-poison-ships-how-international-trade-hazardous-waste-sparked-grassroots-struggle.

Asia Wind Energy Association. 'Country Overview: India.' https://www.asiawind.org/research-data/market-overview/india/.

Copeland, B.J. 'Nouvelle Artificial Intelligence.' *Encyclopaedia Britannica Online*. https://www.britannica.com/technology/nouvelle-artificial-intelligence#ref1070657.

Weinberg, Neal. 'How Amazon Launched the Warehouse Robotics Industry.' TechTarget. 7 August 2020. https://www.techtarget.

com/searchaws/feature/How-Amazon-launched-the-warehouse-robotics-industry.

Giles, Martin. 'The GANfather: The Man Who's Given Machines the Gift of Imagination.' *MIT Technology Review*. 21 February 2018. https://www.technologyreview.com/2018/02/21/145289/the-ganfather-the-man-whos-given-machines-the-gift-of-imagination/.

IIT Madras Alumni Association. 'Remembering Prof. H.N. Mahabala.' https://iitmaa.org/f/remembering-prof-hn-mahabala-15586.

Saint-Dizier, Patrick. 'The Knowledge-Based Computer System Development Program of India: A Review.' Association for the Advancement of Artificial Intelligence. *AI Magazine* 12, no. 2 (1991).

D' Monte, Leslie. 'India Needs More Local Language Models, Datasets to Bridge Digital Divide.' *Mint*. TechTalk column. 15 December 2023. https://www.livemint.com/mint-top-newsletter/techtalk15122023.html.

ET Bureau. 'Fraud Alert! 47% of Indians Have Experienced AI Voice Scams, Says McAfee Survey.' *The Economic Times*. Business news section, panache magazine.17 May 2023. https://economictimes.indiatimes.com/magazines/panache/fraud-alert-47-of-indians-have-experienced-ai-voice-scams/articleshow/100306844.cms.

Dattopant Thengadi National Board for Workers Education & Development. 'Digital Literacy.' Ministry of Labour and Employment, Government of India. https://dtnbwed.cbwe.gov.in/images/upload/Digital-Literacy_3ZNK.pdf.

## READ MORE BY THE AUTHOR

### *UNEARTHED: AN ENVIRONMENTAL HISTORY OF INDEPENDENT INDIA*

Protesting against dams, protecting tigers, hugging trees, saving seeds, making room for elephants, battling mountains of waste, fighting air pollution, coping with soaring temperatures—India and its people have shared a remarkable relationship with the environment. From the Green Revolution to the National Action Plan on Climate Change, *Unearthed: An Environmental History of Independent India* chronicles the country's historical movements and significant green missions since 1947. Interspersed with lots of trivia, tales of eco-heroes and humorous cartoons, this easy-to-read account uncovers the story of a past with the hope that we will rewrite India's future.

READ MORE BY THE AUTHOR

*AFTER MIDNIGHT: A HISTORY OF INDEPENDENT INDIA*

At the time of Independence, few believed that a country made up of British provinces and over 500 princely states could survive as a nation, even for a few years. That a land stripped of its riches, wracked by disease and famine, and divided along tense communal lines could thrive in its aspirations. Yet, in the 75 years since Independence, India has grown beyond anyone's expectation.

How did India get this far? What were the sweeping social, political, scientific, technological, military, environmental and economic developments it witnessed along the way? Interspersed with personal anecdotes, illustrations, infographics, informative timelines and quotes, *After Midnight* revels in the diverse ideas that have come to shape India and offers a multifaceted context to the present. In many ways, this is one of the greatest underdog-beating-the-odds stories in world history, full of blood, sweat, tragedy and triumph.